Cope

HarperCollins*Publishers*

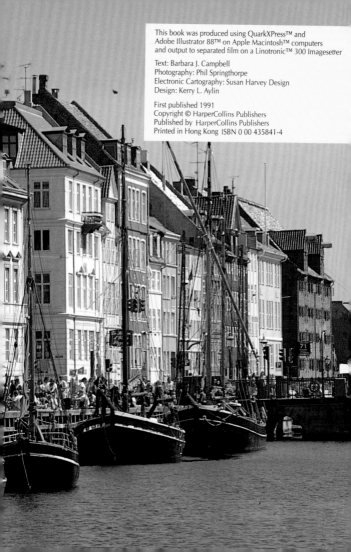

This book was produced using QuarkXPress™ and
Adobe Illustrator 88™ on Apple Macintosh™ computers
and output to separated film on a Linotronic™ 300 Imagesetter

Text: Barbara J. Campbell
Photography: Phil Springthorpe
Electronic Cartography: Susan Harvey Design
Design: Kerry L. Aylin

First published 1991
Copyright © HarperCollins Publishers
Published by HarperCollins Publishers
Printed in Hong Kong ISBN 0 00 435841-4

Your Collins Traveller Guide will help you find your way around your holiday destination quickly and easily. It is split into two sections which are colour-coded:

The blue section provides you with an alphabetical sequence of headings, from **BUILDINGS** to **WALKS** via **EXCURSIONS**, **RESTAURANTS**, **SHOPPING**, etc. Each entry within a topic includes information on how to get there, how much it will cost you, when it will be open and what to expect. Furthermore, every page has its own map showing the position of each item and the nearest landmark. This allows you to orientate yourself quickly and easily in your new surroundings. To find what you want to do – having dinner, visiting a museum, going for a walk or shopping for gifts – simply flick through the blue headings and take your pick!

The red section is an alphabetical list of information. It provides essential facts about places and cultural items – 'What is the Rundetårn?', 'Who was Tycho Brahe?', 'Where is Amager?' – and expands on subjects touched on in the first half of the book. This section also contains practical travel information. It ranges through how to find accommodation, where to hire a car, the variety of eating places and food available, tips on health, information on money, which newspapers are available, how to find a taxi and where the youth hostels are.
It is lively and informative and easy to use. Each band shows the first three letters of the first entry on the page. Simply flick through the bands till you find the entry you need!

All the main entries are also cross-referenced to help you find them. Names in small capitals – **CHILDREN** – tell you that there is more information about the item you are looking for under the topic on children in the first part of the book. So when you read 'see **CHILDREN**' you turn to the blue heading for **CHILDREN**. The instruction 'see **A-Z**', after a word, lets you know that the word has its own entry in the second part of the book. Similarly words in bold type – **Food** – also let you know that there is an entry in the A-Z for the indicated name. In both cases you just look under the appropriate heading in the red section.

Packed full of information and easy to use – you'll always know where you are with your Collins Traveller Guide!

INTRODUCTION

Copenhagen occupies the centre of Danish political, economic and cultural life, and its energy, colour and cosmopolitanism are in marked contrast to the quiet uniformity of the surrounding countryside. *Vive la différence!*

The city began as a small Viking fishing settlement, and is first mentioned in an 11thC saga as 'Havn' ('harbour'). In 1160 Valdemar the Great granted the village and the surrounding land to Bishop Absalon, who built a castle on Slotsholmen where the Christiansborg Palace now stands. Because of its situation on the Sound (Øresund), its excellent harbour and proximity to the vast herring fishing grounds off the coast of Skåne, Copenhagen grew steadily in size and commercial importance during the Middle Ages (in Danish 'København' means 'merchants' harbour'). In 1417 Erik of Pomerania granted royal trading privileges to the city, including the right to levy a sound toll on all vessels passing through Øresund, which placed the city at the centre of Baltic trade. In 1443 it was officially recognized as the Danish capital, and in 1479 became the site of the first Danish university.

During the late 16th and 17thC, the age of absolute monarchy in Europe, Denmark flourished as the leading power in the Baltic, and the glory of successive Danish kings was reflected both in a series of wars waged against the old enemy, Sweden, and in their grandiose building programmes. One Danish monarch in particular, Christian IV (1588-1648), had a passion for town planning and architecture, and was responsible for a large number of construction projects in and around the Danish capital. He replaced his father's modest palace of Frederiksborg, in Hillerød, with the magnificent Renaissance brick structure which stands today (it is now the Danish Museum of National History); he also built the more restrained summer palace of Rosenborg, with its attractive, elegant furnishings, which is now the repository of the Danish crown jewels. Within the old city itself, his architectural legacy includes some of Copenhagen's finest buildings, including the Børsen (Stock Exchange), with its distinctive copper spire of intertwining dragons' tails; the Italianate Tøjhuset (Arsenal), now a museum of military history; and the Rundetårn (Round Tower), originally constructed as an observatory for the University, and up the steps of which Peter the Great is supposed to have ridden on horseback in 1716 (followed

by his wife in a coach!). You can enjoy a magnificent view of the city from the top, perched high above the maze of medieval streets of the old centre below. Another of his building projects, Christianshavn, was designed as a residential area for workers in the shipbuilding trade. The canal, and the grid-like street plan, remind many modern visitors to Copenhagen of Amsterdam, and the monarch was influenced by Dutch design when approving the original plans.

In the 18th and early 19thC the city suffered greatly from a series of disasters, including the plague of 1711-12, in which a third of the population of 60,000 died, and two devastating fires in 1728 and 1795 which destroyed, or partly destroyed, large numbers of buildings, including Helligåndskirke, the city's oldest church, originally founded in 1400 (it was rebuilt, in neo-Renaissance style, in 1880). Fire in 1794 also destroyed much of Christiansborg Palace, built by Christian VI (1730-46). Further damage to the city was sustained in 1801 and 1807 when it was bombarded by the British fleet during the Napoleonic Wars, one notable casualty being Vor Frue Kirke, Copenhagen's cathedral. Despite Denmark's catastrophic support of Napoleon, and its subsequent decline as an international power, the later 19thC was a time of

increasing affluence for the country. The abolition of the sound toll in 1857 encouraged a significant expansion in trade, and improvements in internal communications, industrial growth, and the building of the free port in the 1890s further entrenched Copenhagen at the centre of Danish economic and political life. Considerable changes in the architecture and character of the city accompanied these developments, with the establishment of new districts such as Vesterbro, Nørrebro and Østerbro beyond the old ramparts, which for centuries had enclosed all the main building development. Under the direction of C. F. Hansen, areas of the city were rebuilt in neoclassical style, with wide boulevards punctuated by grandiose buildings such as the Domhuset, formerly the Rådhus and now the Law Courts, and the restored cathedral, Vor Frue Kirke.

This extensive programme of expansion did not, however, spoil the original charm of the city, which remains attractive and easy to explore. Unlike the vast urban sprawls of capitals such as London, Paris or New York, Copenhagen is neat, compact and perfectly flat with the majority of its attractions easily reached on foot and the most interesting sites covered in just a few days' visit.

The old commercial harbour is, today, mostly filled with pleasure cruisers, and is the mooring place of the Danish royal yacht. Nearby, the bronze figure of the Little Mermaid, now the emblem of the city, reclines on her rock, looking wistfully out to sea. Behind her stands the attractive Churchill Park which contains the Museum of the Danish Resistance Movement, where brave acts of opposition to Nazi occupation during World War II are documented. Nyhavn (New Harbour), a picturesque area with outdoor cafés, old wooden sailing vessels moored along the canalside, expensive antique shops and fish restaurants, is an ideal spot for people-watching on a sunny day. Strøget ('Strolling'), a series of streets filled with pedestrians, cyclists and street entertainers, is another major attraction with its many cafés, restaurants and shops. (Some of the latter, such as Illums Bolighus and the Royal Porcelain Factory, specialize in famous Danish design.) Much of the city's life is also focused on Copenhagen's largest square, Kongens Nytorv, which features an equestrian statue of Christian V and is the site both of the Royal Theatre and of the Charlottenborg, home of the Royal Academy of Art and the Danish Ballet; whilst Christiansborg, on the island of Slotsholmen, is the administrative centre of the country and contains the Danish parliament, government offices, various museums and the ruins of Bishop Absalon's original castle. Art lovers may want to head for the State Museum of Art, housing paintings by numerous European Masters; the charming Hirschsprung Collection of 19thC Danish paintings and sculptures; the Ny Carlsberg Glyptotek, containing the family's collection of art dating from the Etruscan period to modern times; and the Thorvaldsen Museum, where works by the country's most prolific and celebrated sculptor are gathered. In summer, the less cerebral delights of the famous Tivoli Gardens provide amusement and entertainment for young and old alike.

All in all, Copenhagen constitutes one of the most delightful capitals in Europe – an attractive and harmonious city of wide, uncluttered horizons and hospitable and charming inhabitants.

AMALIENBORG SLOT Amalienborg Plads.
❑ Changing of the Guard daily 1200. Palace not open to the public.
Bus 1, 2, 6, 8, 10, 15E.
*Four identical 18thC rococo mansions set around an elegant square,
constitute the royal residence. See* **WALK 4, A-Z.**

BØRSEN Børsgade.
❑ Not open to the public. Bus 1, 2, 6, 8, 10, 15E.
*The old Stock Exchange building. Its most distinctive feature is the long
copper roof topped by a spire consisting of the intertwined tails of four
dragons, reputedly designed by Christian IV (see* **A-Z**). *See* **WALKS 2 & 3**.

CHRISTIANSBORG SLOT Slotsholmen.
❑ See **Christiansborg Slot**. Bus 1, 2, 5, 8, 9, 10, 31, 37, 43.
*The palace is the official seat of power in Denmark. Contains the Danish
Parliament, royal reception rooms and 12thC castle remains. See* **A-Z.**

DET KONGELIGE BIBLIOTEK (ROYAL LIBRARY) Christians
Brygge 8 (entrance from Rigsdagsgården).
❑ 0900-1900 Mon.-Fri., 1000-1900 Sat. (June-Aug.); 0900-1900 Mon.
& Fri., 0900-2100 Tue., Wed., Thu., 1000-1900 Sat. (Jan.-May, Sep.-
Dec.). Bus 1, 2, 5, 6, 8, 10, 15E. ❑ Free.
*Founded by King Frederik III in 1670, this is one of the largest collec-
tions in Europe, with over 3.3 million volumes. See* **WALK 3.**

RÅDHUS (TOWN HALL) Rådhuspladsen.
❑ 1000-1500 Mon.-Fri. (tours of building and tower available). S-train
to Vesterport; bus 1, 6, 8, 14, 19, 28, 30, 34, 41, 64, 71E. ❑ 10kr.
*Designed and built by Martin Nyrop between 1849 and 1905. Contains
Jens Olsen's World Clock (see* **A-Z**). *See* **A-Z.**

RUNDETÅRN (ROUND TOWER) Købmagergade.
❑ 1000-1700 Mon.-Sat., 1200-1600 Sun. (Apr.-Oct.); 1000-2000 Mon.-
Sat., 1200-2000 Sun. (June-Aug.). S-train to Nørreport. ❑ 10kr/4kr.
*Built between 1637-42 as part of the university complex with Trinitatis
Kirke (see* **CHURCHES**). *The tower is 37 m high. See* **A-Z.**

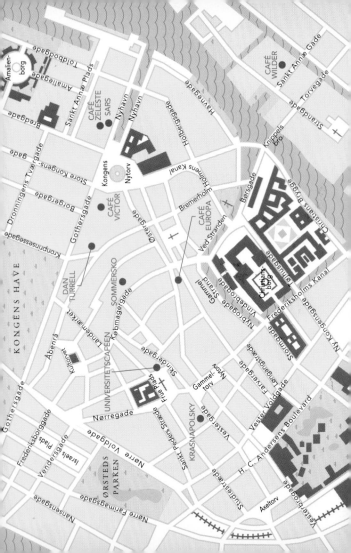

KRASNAPOLSKY Vestergade 10.
❏ 0900-0200. Bus 1, 6, 8, 14, 19, 28, 30, 34, 41, 64, 71E.
Style-conscious café, high-tech interior. Live music every second Mon.

DAN TURRELL Store Regnegade 3-5.
❏ 1100-0200 Mon.-Sat., 1200-0200 Sun. Bus 7, 43.
This café attracts a Bohemian, literary clientele. There is a small restaurant which serves inexpensive meals.

SOMMERSKO Kronprinsensgade 6.
❏ 0900-0100. Bus 43.
Popular café, with bistro restaurant, serves an excellent breakfast.

UNIVERSITETSCAFEEN Fiolstræde 2.
❏ 1000-0430 Mon.-Sat., 1700-0430 Sun. Bus 4, 6, 8, 14, 19, 28, 30.
Student hang-out, serving inexpensive snacks.

CAFÉ VICTOR Ny Østergade 8.
❏ 0900-0200 Mon.-Sat. Bus 7, 43.
The place to see and be seen in, very busy at weekends.

CAFÉ WILDER Wildersgade 56.
❏ 0900-0200 Mon.-Fri., 1200-0200 Sat., Sun. Bus 2, 8, 9, 31, 37.
Cosy corner café in fashionable Christianshavn (see WALK 2, **A-Z**).

SARS Nyhavn 15.
❏ 1100-0100 Mon.-Fri. (closed Tue.), 0900-0100 Sat., Sun. Bus 1, 6.
Bright and cheerful basement café serving good, inexpensive food.

CAFÉ EUROPA Amagertorv 1.
❏ 0900-2400 Mon.-Sat., 1000-2400 Sun. Bus 28, 29, 41.
In summer this is an outdoor café and an ideal spot for people-watching.

CAFÉ ZELESTE Store Strandstræde 6.
❏ 1200-2400 Mon.-Tue., 1200-0100 Wed.-Sat. Bus 1, 6, 9, 10.
Smart café with a pretty courtyard. Medium-priced restaurant upstairs.

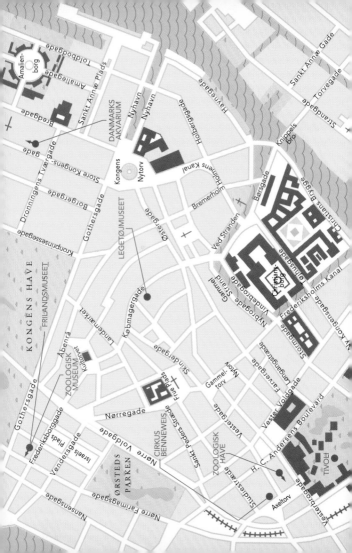

CIRKUS BENNEWEIS Axeltorv.
❏ 2000 Tue.-Fri., 1600 & 2000 Sat., 1600 Sun. (1 June-16 Aug.); 2000 Mon. (17 Aug.-end Oct.). S-train to Vesterport or Central Station; bus 1, 6, 8, 14, 16, 28, 29, 41. ❏ Tel: 33144443 (1200-2000) for price info.
This 100-year-old circus is the largest in Europe. See **Circus**.

LEGETØJMUSEET (TOY MUSEUM) Valkendorfsgade 13.
❏ 0900-1500 Mon.-Thu., 1000-1600 Sat., Sun. S-train to Nørreport.
❏ 20kr, child 10kr.
One hundred years of toys, exhibited in bright attic rooms.

ZOOLOGISK HAVE Roskildevej 32.
❏ 0900-1700 Mon.-Fri., 0900-1800 Sat., Sun. Bus 28, 39, 41.
❏ 35kr, child 16kr.
An attractive zoo with largely cage-free enclosures. See **A-Z**.

TIVOLI Main entrance on Vesterbrogade (also access via Bernstorffsgade, Dentes Plads, Rådhuspladsen).
❏ 1000-2400 (end April-mid Sep.), amusements till 1130. S-train to Vesterport; bus 1, 6, 8, 10, 11, 12, 13. ❏ 28kr, child 14kr, *turpas* 115kr.
A magical pleasure park with a variety of attractions. See **A-Z**.

ZOOLOGISK MUSEUM Universitetsparken 15.
❏ 1000-1700 May-Sep.; 1300-1700 Mon.-Fri., 1000-1700 Sat., Sun. & hol. (Oct.-April). Bus 18, 24, 43, 84, 184. ❏ Free.
Natural-history museum, with children's attractions. See **A-Z**.

FRILANDSMUSEET 54 km north of Copenhagen.
❏ 1000-1700 15 April-30 Sep. S-train to Sorgenfri, then a short walk.
❏ 15kr, child 5kr.
A display of historic Danish cottages and houses. See **EXCURSION 1**.

DANMARKS AKVARIUM Off Strandvejen, Charlottenlund.
❏ 1000-1800 1 Mar.-31 Oct. S-train from Vesterport to Charlottenlund, then a short walk. ❏ 30kr, child 15kr.
One of Europe's most impressive aquariums. See **EXCURSION 1**.

HOLMENS KIRKE Holmens Kanal.
❑ 0900-1400 Mon.-Fri., 0900-1200 Sat. Bus 1, 2, 6, 9, 10, 31. ❑ Free.
Surrounded by water, this is the church of the Danish royal family.

TRINITATIS KIRKE Købmagergade.
❑ 0900-1500. S-train to Nørreport. ❑ Free.
Neo-Gothic church with an ornate interior. See **Rundetårn**.

VOR FRELSERS KIRKE Sankt Annæ Gade.
❑ 0900-1530 Mon.-Sat.,1200-1530 Sun. (June-Aug.). Bus 2, 8, 9, 31,
37. ❑ Tower: 10kr, child 4kr.
Baroque church with green-and-gold spiral tower. See **WALK 2**, **A-Z**.

VOR FRUE KIRKE/DOMKIRKE Frue Plads, Nørregade.
❑ 0900-1700. S-train to Nørreport; bus 5. ❑ Free.
*This elegant neoclassical church is Copenhagen's cathedral. It is deco-
rated with sculptures by Bertel Thorvaldsen. See* **A-Z**.

ALEXANDER NEWSKY KIRKE Bredgade 53 (tel: 31180306).
❑ Service 1000 Sun.; by arrangement for groups. Bus 1, 6, 9. ❑ Free.
*The church of Copenhagen's Russian Orthodox community and easily
recognizable by its three gold onion domes. See* **WALK 4**.

SANKT ANSGAR KIRKE Bredgade 64.
❑ 0730-1700. Bus 1, 6, 9. ❑ Free.
Denmark's Roman Catholic cathedral, designed in neo-Gothic style.

CHRISTIANS KIRKE Strandgade.
❑ 0800-1700. Bus 2, 8, 9, 31, 37. ❑ Free.
Rococo church designed by Nicolai Eigtved. See **WALK 2**.

SANKT PETRI KIRKE Sankt Peders Stræde.
❑ Guided tours by arrangement 1000-1100 Tue., Wed.; 1100-1200
Sun., tel: 31133834. S-train to Nørreport. ❑ Free.
*15thC Gothic church with later Renaissance additions. It is currently
undergoing major renovation work.*

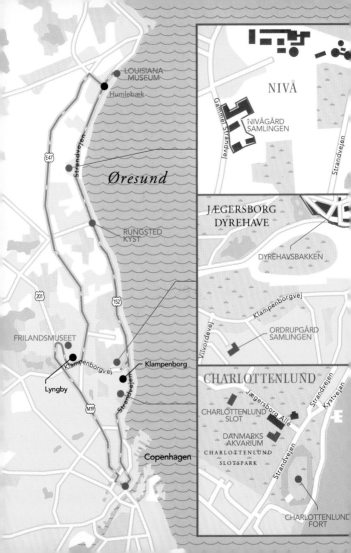

LOUISIANA
MUSEUM
Humlebæk

E47

Strandvejen

Øresund

RUNGSTED
KYST

201

152

FRILANDSMUSEET

Klampenborgvej

Lyngby

Klampenborg

M19

Strandvejen

Copenhagen

NIVÅ

Gammel Strandvej

NIVÅGÅRD
SAMLINGEN

Strandvejen

JÆGERSBORG
DYREHAVE

DYREHAVSBAKKEN

Klampenborgvej

Vilvordevej

ORDRUPGÅRD
SAMLINGEN

CHARLOTTENLUND

Strandvejen

Kystvejen

Jægersborg Allé

CHARLOTTENLUND
SLOT

DANMARKS
AKVARIUM

CHARLOTTENLUND
SLOTSPARK

Strandvejen

CHARLOTTENLUND
FORT

EXCURSION 1

Charlottenlund-Humlebæk

A one-day trip to Charlottenlund, Bakken amusement park, the Louisiana Museum, Frilandsmuseet, and the burial place of writer Karen Blixen.

Take route 152 (Strandvejen) out of Copenhagen.

9 km – Charlottenlund. Overlooking the beach to the right are the remains of Charlottenlund Fort. Although the actual fortifications are no longer visible, the extensive earthworks are. Some of these now form part of the camp site at the fort. Just beyond the fort, set back off Strandvejen, is Danmarks Akvarium, featuring impressive aquatic displays (see **CHILDREN**). Park at the aquarium and walk through the park to the palace, Charlottenlund Slot. This graceful mansion (1890) now houses the Danish Fisheries and Maritime Research Unit. Return to Strandvejen, and carry on towards Klampenborg, then turn left onto Dyrehavevej (opposite Bellevue beach – follow the sign for Dyrehavsbakken).

11 km – Bakken. There has been a fair at the southern end of the Jægersborg Dyrehave (Deer Park) for 400 years, and it is popular with the Danes for family outings. There are rides, amusement arcades and fast-food stalls, as well as restaurants and cafés, and a variety theatre set in a huge tent (1 April-31 Aug.; free). You can stroll in the deer park, or hire a horse-drawn carriage and ride in comfort. Close to the Deer Park, at Vilvordevej 110, is the Ordrupgård Samlingen (Ordrupgård Collection), donated to the state in 1953 by Danish businessman Wilhelm Hansen, which includes works by the French Impressionists, and other 19thC French and Danish artists (1300-1700, 1900-2200 Wed., all year). Return to Strandvejen and continue north.

23 km – Rungsted Kyst. Just opposite the yachting marina sits the former home of Danish author Karen Blixen – Rungsted Lund (see **Blixen**). Although the house is not open to the public, Rungsted Lund Park (now a bird sanctuary) is, and the writer is buried in the grounds here under a large beech tree.

29 km – Nivå. Turn left off Strandvejen onto Gammel Strandvej and drive about 1 km to visit the Nivågård Samlingen (Nivågård Collection). Landowner Johannes Hage's collection of Italian Renaissance, Dutch 17thC and Danish 19thC art includes works by Bellini, Rembrandt and Rubens (1300-1600 Tue.-Fri. (20 May-31 Dec.); 1200-1700 Sat., Sun. (all year); 15kr, child free). Return to Strandvejen, and head north.

33 km – Humlebæk. About 1 km north of the centre of town lies the Louisiana Modern Art Museum which was opened in 1958. All the exhibits date from after World War II and the museum contains work by

Warhol, Picasso and Giacometti. There are also Henry Moore sculptures among the trees and shrubs of the grounds which overlook the waters of Øresund. The museum is open 1000-1700 (Wed. till 2200) all year, and costs 40kr, child free. Return to Humlebæk centre, then turn right into Fredensborgvej. Drive 2.5 km to join the Helsingør motorway (E47), and follow the signs for København (Copenhagen). Drive south for 20 km and exit at Lyngby Ø/C junction, then drive along Klampenborgvej towards Lyngby. From Lyngby centre, turn right and go along Lyngby Hovedgade, which becomes Kongevejen, for 2 km.

54 km – Frilandsmuseet. This open-air museum features about 100 old cottages and houses from all over Denmark and from various historical periods, transplanted into rural surroundings. The houses are furnished in authentic period style, and equipped with household implements and working tools of the time (see **CHILDREN**). From Frilandsmuseet, take route 201, joining up with motorway 19, to return to Copenhagen city centre (13 km).

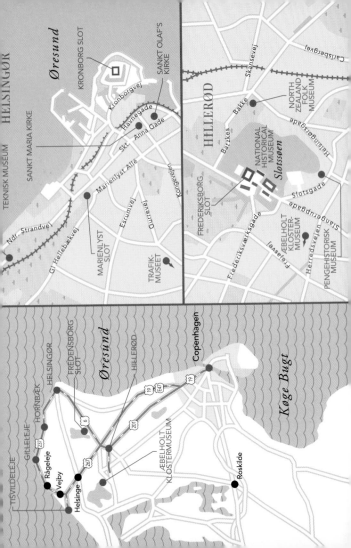

EXCURSION 2

North Zealand Coast

A one-day tour visiting Hillerød, Fredensborg, Helsingør, and the north coast of Zealand.

Take route 19 out of Copenhagen following the signs for Helsingør, and then take the 201 through Lyngby.

36 km – Hillerød. The town grew up around its main feature, Frederiksborg Slot (Castle), an impressive brick Renaissance edifice situated at the end of a large lake. It was built by Christian IV between 1602 and 1625 on the site of an earlier palace of Frederik II. Frederiksborg was destroyed by fire in 1859, but rebuilt in the original style. The rebuilding was masterminded and largely funded by J. C. Jacobsen of the Carlsberg Brewery (see **A-Z**), and the castle is today part of the Carlsberg Foundation. It also houses Denmark's National Historical Museum (1000-1600 1-30 April, 1000-1700 1 May-30 Sep., 1000-1600 1-31 Oct.; 20k, child 5kr).

Other attractions in Hillerød include the Pengehistorisk Museum (Museum of Money); the North Zealand Folk Museum, which concentrates on the agricultural history of North Zealand; and the Æbelholt Klostermuseum, the ruins of a medieval abbey. From the town centre, drive north along Holmegårdsvej and continue along Fredensborgvej. Just as you enter the town limits, turn left along Slotsgade and take route 6 out of Hillerød.

44 km – Fredensborg Slot. The castle is the spring and autumn residence of the Danish royal family, built in 1722 in Italian style for Frederik IV, and subsequently much altered and extended. Fredensborg Slotspark (the Castle Park) is an elegant formal park which was laid out in 1780 (open to the public all year round); Marmorhaven (the Marble Garden) is the Royal family's private garden (open mid-June to early Sep.). Continue on route 6, which joins with the motorway (E47).

59 km – Helsingør (see **A-Z**). A busy, prosperous port at the entrance to Øresund. The town was originally established in the 15thC as a control post for levying the newly introduced sound toll which had to be paid by every boat wishing to pass through the narrow stretch of water dividing this part of Denmark from Sweden. Many Swedes take advantage of the short ferry trip across to Denmark where they can buy goods – especially alcohol – cheaper than in their own country.

Nearby is Kronborg Slot – a large brooding castle in a dramatic setting overlooking the Sound. Although famous as the setting for Shakespeare's *Hamlet*, it is uncertain whether the playwright himself ever visited Kronborg. The earlier, 15thC castle on this site was replaced by a larger fortress in 1585. This castle burnt down in 1629 and the present building was completed in 1637. The Renaissance chapel, containing notable ornate wood carvings, is the only section which survived the fire of 1629. The Casements (dungeons) are suitably damp, cold and dark. Down here you can see the statue of Holger the Dane. This huge Viking sleeps leaning on his sword and shield, ready to wake and answer the call when needed to come to Denmark's aid. The Royal Apartments are a series of large, beautifully proportioned rooms, many enjoying spectacular views of the Sound.

Also of interest in Helsingør are: Sankt Olaf's Kirke, Helsingør's cathedral, founded c.1200, and completed in the 16thC; Sankt Maria Kirke and the Carmelite Cloisters, a well-preserved 15thC Gothic complex, which contains 17thC frescos; Marienlyst Slot (Castle), a fine neoclassi-

cal building, initially built as a summer residence by Frederik II, containing beautifully preserved Louis Seize interiors; Danmarks Teknisk Museum, an exhibition of natural science and technology, demonstrating various types of machines, large and small; and Traffic Hall, on the other side of Helsingør (Ole Rømersvej), which is part of the Teknisk Museum and houses the Trafikmuseet (Museum of Transport). Drive north on route 237 (Nordre Standvej) out of Helsingør to visit some of the picturesque fishing villages along the coast of North Zealand.

73 km – Hornbæk. One of the oldest fishing villages in North Zealand.

87 km – Gilleleje. A busy, working, fishing port, which also boasts some of the prettiest and most brightly painted cottages. The drive to Tisvildeleje will take you through Rågeleje and Vejby and passes some beautiful countryside on the way.

98 km – Tisvildeleje. Along the length of this coastline lies a wide, unbroken stretch of fine white sand with large sand dunes.

Pick up route 267 back to Hillerød, where it joins route 19 to Copenhagen (54 km).

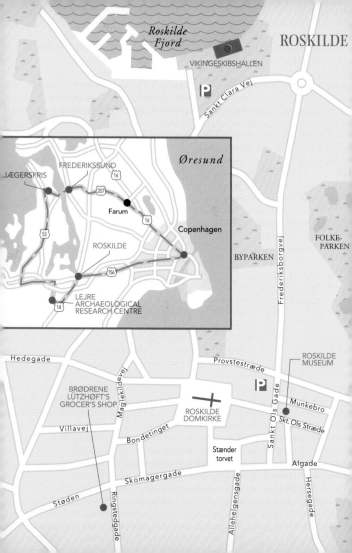

Roskilde *Fjord*

ROSKILDE

VIKINGESKIBSHALLEN

Sankt Clara Vej

Øresund

JÆGERSPRIS

FREDERIKSSUND
16

207

Farum

16

Copenhagen

53

ROSKILDE

156

14

LEJRE
ARCHAEOLOGICAL
RESEARCH CENTRE

FOLKE-
PARKEN

BYPARKEN

Frederiksborgvej

Hedegade

Provstestræde

ROSKILDE
MUSEUM

BRØDRENE
LÜTZHØFT'S
GROCER'S SHOP

Maglekildevej

ROSKILDE
DOMKIRKE

Sankt Ols Gade

Munkebro

Skt. Ols Stræde

Villavej

Bondetinget

Stænder
torvet

Algade

Støden

Ringstedgade

Skomagergade

Allehelgensgade

Hersegade

EXCURSION 3

Roskilde

A one-day trip inland to the historic town of Roskilde.

From Copenhagen city centre, drive along Vesterbrogade, then follow Roskildevej (route 156).

35 km – Roskilde (see **A-Z**). This is one of the oldest towns on Zealand. Roskilde Cathedral, in Domkirkestræde, was established by Bishop Absalon in the 1170s. The oldest parts of the cathedral are built in a mixture of Romanesque and Gothic styles. It has been the burial place of all Danish monarchs since 1559, and a new side chapel has been added for each successive monarch, so that the cathedral is now very much a hotch-potch of different styles. Notable features include the carved wooden choir stalls from the 14thC; Frederik V's neoclassical side chapel; and the clockwork model of St. George and the dragon accompanied by the Danish folk figures of Kirsten Kimer and Per Døver (the best time to see the model in action is at 1200 noon).

There are also several interesting museums in Roskilde which are worth visiting. The Vikingeskibshallen (Viking Ship Museum) is housed in a custom-built complex at the head of Roskilde Fjord. It contains the remains and reconstructions of five Viking ships which had sunk in Roskilde Fjord and were salvaged in 1962 (open 0900-1700 April-Oct., 1000-1600 Nov.-Mar.; 5kr, child free). The local Roskilde Museum contains reconstructions of typical rooms from different periods in the town's history, and also features a Museum of Childhood. Brødrene Lützhøft's Grocer's Shop, run by Roskilde Museum, is a working shop, preserved exactly as it would have been in the years 1910-20. From Roskilde take route 14 southwest towards Lejre.

43 km – Lejre Archaeological Research Centre. Set in reconstructed settlements from early Danish history, the centre promotes research into the daily life of Stone-Age people and other prehistoric cultures. From Lejre, take route 155 and drive round the south end of Roskilde fjord, then join route 53 northwards along Horns Herred.

74 km – Jægerspris. Jægerspris Slot was originally the 13thC castle of Abrahamstrup, enlarged by Christian IV, and renamed in 1677 (guided tours hourly). From Jægerspris, cross the fjord (on route 53).

80 km – Frederikssund. The setting every summer for a series of Viking plays. Return to Copenhagen on route 207 and route 16 at Farum.

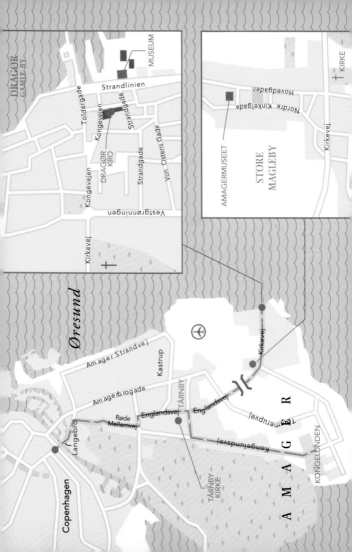

A one-day trip exploring the attractive area south of Copenhagen.

From Copenhagen city centre cross Langebro (bridge) to the island of
Amager (see **A-Z**). Follow Amager Boulevard, then turn right onto
Amager Fælledvej, and continue on Røde Mellemvej. Turn left on
Vejlands Allé and right on Englandsvej. The road is clearly signposted
to Kastrup Airport and Dragør.

Although within only a 20-minute drive of
the city, this area seems hardly to have
changed in the past 200 years. Amager was
colonized 400 years ago by Dutch immi-
grants, who cultivated the soil on this
65-sq.-km island and turned it into a large
market garden, supplying vegetables to the
citizens of Copenhagen. You will see many
reminders of these Dutch residents in the
style of the local buildings.

Drive along Englandsvej to the village of
Tårnby, which contains Tårnby Kirke, the
oldest church on Amager. The oldest parts
of the church date from the 12thC. Inside
there is a 12thC font hewn from one mas-
sive block of granite, frescoes from the first
half of the 14thC and a carved pulpit and
pews of oak from the late 16th and 17thC.

If you feel like taking a woodland walk, leave Englandsvej just beyond
Tårnby, drive along Løjtegårdsvej, then turn left into Kongelundsvej.
This leads to Kongelunden wood, laid out in 1830 and formerly a pos-
session of the Danish royal family.

From Tårnby it is only a matter of a few minutes' drive along
Englandsvej to Store Magleby. This attractive village looks very much as
it did in the 17thC. The cottages are brightly painted, and many of them
have Danish-style thatched roofs. The church was built in 1611 by the
Dutch community, although there has been a church on this spot since
the Middle Ages. The Amagermuseet (Amager Museum) in Store
Magleby which occupies two old farms in the main street, is worth a

visit as the exhibits on display, including reconstructions of typical peasant rooms, will help to give you a picture of how life used to be on Amager. Continuing along Kirkevej from Store Magleby will bring you to the village of Dragør. Follow the signs for Dragør Gamle By (Dragør Old Town) and drive straight down to the harbour where there are parking spaces.

You can now wander through the cobbled streets of what is certainly one of the most charming villages in Denmark. The oldest building in the village is the former guildhall, now the museum, set beside the harbour, although most of the houses in Dragør date from the beginning of the 19thC. As you explore you can see how much pride the residents of Dragør take in their homes – all are beautifully painted and maintained. Even the town shops are careful not to present a brash aspect, and blend in extremely well. Dragør Kro, the village inn, is beautifully preserved and has a pleasant courtyard which patrons can enjoy in good weather. What saves the village from becoming overly cosy, and what gives it a special extra dimension, is its position beside the sea. At the harbour itself, there is a superb view of the Sound, and the Swedish coast across the water. This is a busy channel, with regular ferries going backwards and forwards between Dragør and Sweden. From the vantage point of the harbour, it is easy to see why Dragør, so strategically placed, was at one time one of Denmark's most important ports. Return to Copenhagen by the same route.

ORLOGSMUSEET Overgade oven Vandet 58.
❏ 1200-1600 Tue.-Sun. (April-Sep.). Bus 2, 8, 31. ❏ 20kr, child 10kr.
Danish Navy museum, housed in a former naval hospital. See **WALK 2**.

NY CARLSBERG GLYPTOTEK Dantes Plads.
❏ 1000-1600 Tue.-Sun. (May-Aug.); 1200-1500 Tue.-Sat., 1000-1600
Sun. (Sep.-April). Bus 1, 2, 5, 10, 14, 16, 28, 29. ❏ 15kr, child free.
*This large museum comprises two main sections: antiquities, and a large
collection of sculpture and Impressionist paintings. See* **A-Z**.

KØBENHAVNS BYMUSEUM Vesterbrogade 59.
❏ 1000-1600 Tue.-Sun. (May-Sep.); 1300-1600 Tue.-Sun. (Oct.-April).
Bus 6, 16, 28, 41. ❏ Free.
Contains exhibits illustrating the history of Copenhagen.

DAVIDS SAMLINGEN Kronprinsessegade.
❏ 1300-1600 Tue.-Sun. Bus 7, 10, 43. ❏ Free.
Furniture, silver, porcelain and Islamic art, in a 19thC townhouse.

FRIHEDSMUSEET Churchillparken.
❏ 1000-1600 Tue.-Sat., 1000-1700 Sun. (May-mid-Sep.); 1100-1500
Tue.-Sat., 1100-1600 Sun. (mid-Sep.-April). Bus 1, 8, 9. ❏ Free.
Museum of the Danish Resistance movement. See **WALKS 1 & 4**, **A-Z**.

HIRSCHSPRUNGS SAMLINGEN Stockholmsgade 20.
❏ 1300-1600 Wed.-Sun. (& 1900-2200 Wed.). Bus 10, 14, 24. ❏ Free.
Collection of 19thC Danish art in a neoclassical building. See **A-Z**.

NATIONALMUSEET Frederiksholms Kanal 12.
❏ 1000-1600 Tue.-Sun. Bus 1, 2, 5, 6, 10. ❏ Free.
Extensive museum of Danish social and cultural history. See **A-Z**.

KUNSTINDUSTRIMUSEET (APPLIED ART) Bredgade 68.
❏ 1000-1600 Tue.-Sun. Bus 1, 6, 9. ❏ 12kr Sat., Sun. (& Tue.-Fri. in
July-Aug.), otherwise free.
Decorative art from the Middle Ages to 1980s. Oriental arts and crafts.

STATENS MUSEUM FOR KUNST Sølvgade 48-50.
❑ 1000-1630 Tue.-Sun. Bus 10, 24, 43, 84. ❑ Free.
*Houses a permanent exhibition of contemporary Danish paintings, as
well as the works of many famous international artists. See* **A-Z**.

ROYAL COPENHAGEN PORCELAIN MUSEUM Smalleg. 45.
❑ Organized tours 1000, 1100, 1300, 1400 Mon.-Fri. (June-Sep.);
1000, 1100, Mon.-Fri. (Oct.-May). Bus 1, 14. ❑ Free.
Examples of work from the Royal Copenhagen factory.

ROSENBORG SLOT Øster Voldgade 4A.
❑ 1100-1500 May, Sep.-Oct.; 1000-1500 June-Aug.; 1100-1300 Tue.,
Fri., till 1400 Sun. (Oct.-April). S-train to Nørreport. ❑ 25kr, child 5kr.
Summer palace of Christian IV. Contains the crown jewels. See **A-Z**.

TØJHUSMUSEET (ARSENAL MUSEUM) Tøjhusgade 3.
❑ 1300-1600 Tue.-Sat., 1100-1600 Sun. Bus 1, 2, 5, 6, 8, 10. ❑ Free.
Includes weapons and militaria from the 15thC to the modern day.

TEATERMUSEET Christiansborg Ridebane 19.
❑ 1400-1600 Wed., Fri., Sun. Bus 1, 2, 5, 6, 8. ❑ 15kr, child 5kr.
Located in the former royal theatre, built over the royal stables.

THORVALDSENS MUSEUM Porthusgade 2.
❑ 1000-1700. Bus 1, 2, 6, 8, 10, 28, 29, 41. ❑ Free.
Displays the works of sculptor Bertil Thorvaldsen. See **WALK 3**, **A-Z**.

LOUIS TUSSAUD'S WAX MUSEUM H. C. Andersens Blvd 22.
❑ 1000-1930 1-25 April & 11-30 Sep., 1000-2300 26 April-10 Sep.
Bus 1, 6, 8, 14, 19, 28, 30, 34, 41, 64, 71E. ❑ 39kr, child 16kr.
Models of the famous and infamous. Good Chamber of Horrors.

HOLOGRAFISK MUSEUM H. C. Andersens Boulevard 22.
❑ 1000-2400 May-Sep.; 1000-1830 Mon.-Fri., 1000-2000 Sat., Sun.
(Oct.-April). Bus 1, 6. ❑ 28kr/18kr (May-Sep.), 30kr/ 22kr (Oct.-April).
A stunning exhibition of three-dimensional pictures.

CLUB PRIVE

ANNABELS

Toldbodgade

Esplanaden

Kongelsgade

Bredgade

Grønningen

Store Kongensgade

Borgergade

Kronprinsessegade

Nyhavn
Nyhavn

Havnegade

Nytorv

Kongens

Øvregaden ved Vandet

Strandgade

Øvregaden oven Vandet
Prinsessegade

Amager Boulevard

MUSIKCAFEEN

Øster Voldgade

ØSTER

KONGENS
HAVE

Gothersgade

Købmagergade

Øster Søgade

Øster Farimagsgade

MONTMARTRE

Nørregade

Nørre Voldgade

LA FONTAINE

Vester Voldgade

Peder Skrams Gade

Langebro

Christians Brygge

Kalvebod Brygge

Sortedams Sø

Nørre Farimagsgade

Nørre Søgade

PAN
CAFÉ
& DISCO

Vesterdgade

H. C. Andersens Boulevard

Peder Hvitfeldts

Bernstorffsgade

Peblinge Dosering

Peblinge Sø

Nørrebrogade

Sct. Jørgens Sø

Vester Søgade

Vodroffsvej

Gammel Kongevej

BENWEBSTERS

FELLINI

Vesterbrogade

Istedgade

Aboulevard

H. C. Ørsteds Vej

Rolighedsvej

Bülowsvej

MUSIKCAFEEN Rådhusstræde 13.
❏ 2100-0200. Bus 28, 29, 41. ❏ 60-100kr.
Club featuring Danish and international rock and jazz music. It is located in the Huset *(The House) complex – an alternative youth centre.*

PAN CAFÉ & DISCO Knabrostræde 3.
❏ 1200-0300 Mon.-Thu., 1200-0400 Fri., 1130-0500 Sat., 1300-0300 Sun. Bus 5, 28, 29, 41. ❏ Café free; disco varies from free up to 50kr.
Part of a gay complex which includes a bookshop and contact centre.

FELLINI SAS Royal Hotel, Hammerichsgade 1.
❏ 2200-0300 Mon.-Wed., 2200-0430 Thu.-Sat. S-train to Vesterport.
❏ 60kr.
Sophisticated and expensive nightspot featuring an exotic cabaret.

ANNABELS Lille Kongensgade 19.
❏ 2300-0500 Thu.-Sat. Bus 28, 29, 41, 43. ❏ 50kr.
Disco catering for sophisticated over 30s. Plush decor, and expensive.

LA FONTAINE Kompagnistræde 11.
❏ 2200-0500 Tue.-Sat. Bus 28, 29, 41. ❏ Free.
Small, atmospheric jazz club. Live music every evening from 2300.

MONTMARTRE Nørregade 41.
❏ 2000-0100 Mon.-Thu., 2000-0500 Fri., Sat. S-train to Nørreport.
❏ 80-100kr.
Important jazz venue, featuring many big international artists.

BENWEBSTERS Vestergade 7.
❏ 1800-0500. Bus 1, 6, 8, 14, 19, 28, 30, 34, 41, 64, 71E. ❏ Free if eating, otherwise 30-50kr.
Jazz club and restaurant. Live jazz every night. Reasonably priced menu.

CLUB PRIVE Ny Østergade 14.
❏ Disco 2100-0300 Tue.-Thu., 2300-0500 Fri., Sat. Bus 7. ❏ 50kr.
Chic, up-market disco. Clientele in mid-20s to early 30s.

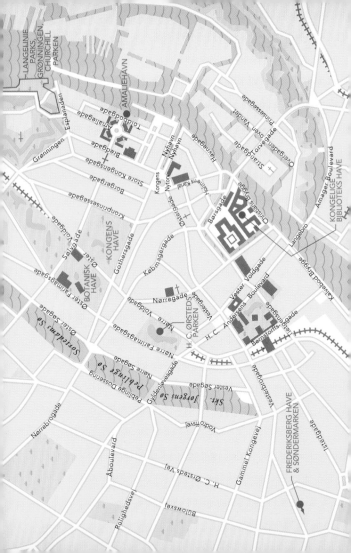

KONGENS HAVE Gothersgade.
❑ Dawn-dusk. S-train to Nørreport; bus 10, 14, 40, 43. ❑ Free.
Large park designed by Christian IV (see **A-Z***) at the same time as*
Rosenborg Slot (see **A-Z***). Contains a statue of H. C. Andersen.*

BOTANISK HAVE Gothersgade & Øster Voldgade.
❑ 0830-1600. S-train to Nørreport; bus 14, 40, 43 ❑ Free.
A beautifully laid out garden. Particularly notable are the Palm House
and the huge rockery.

FREDERIKSBERG HAVE & SØNDERMARKEN Pile Alle.
❑ Dawn-dusk. Bus 6, 18, 28, 41. ❑ Free.
Originally the gardens of Frederiksberg Palace (see **Frederiksberg Slot***),*
they are particularly lovely in spring, and contain, among other things, a
Chinese Pavilion recently renovated and now open to the public.

AMALIEHAVEN Toldbodgade.
❑ 24hr. Bus 1, 6, 9, 10, then a short walk. ❑ Free.
A modern garden, donated to the city by shipping magnate, A. P. Møller.
It contains a spectacular fountain and distinctive sculpture. See **WALK 4***.*

H. C. ØRSTEDS PARKEN Nørre Voldgade.
❑ Dawn-dusk. S-train to Nørreport; bus 5, 14, 16, 40. ❑ Free.
A peaceful spot between the busy thoroughfares of Nørre Voldgade and
Nørre Farimagsgade, dedicated to the Danish physicist.

KONGELIGE BIBLIOTEKS HAVE Rigsdagsgården Christiansborg.
❑ Dawn-dusk. Bus 1, 2, 5, 6, 8, 10. ❑ Free.
The smallest, prettiest and most secluded of the public gardens, lying
between Christiansborg Palace and the Royal Library. See **WALK 3***.*

**LANGELINIE PARKS, GRØNNINGEN, CHURCHILL-
PARKEN** Langelinie, Esplanaden.
❑ Dawn-dusk. Bus 1, 6, 9. ❑ Free.
A series of parks and gardens which stretch along the harbour side. The
statue of the Little Mermaid (see **WALK 1***,* **A-Z***) sits on Langelinie.*

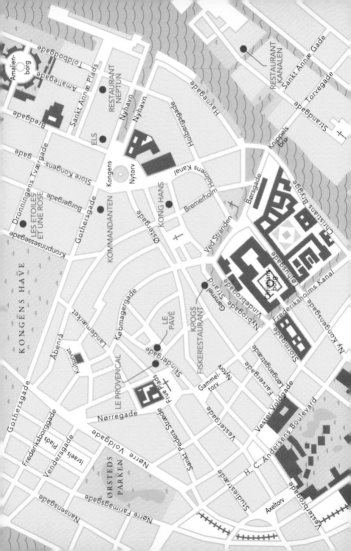

Amalien-
borg

Toldbodgade

Amaliegade

Bredgade

Sankt Annæ Plads

RESTAURANT
NEPTUN

Nyhavn

Nyhavn

RESTAURANT
KANALEN

Sankt Annæ Gade

Torvegade

Strandgade

Havnegade

ELS

Store Kongensgade

Dronningens Tværgade

Borgergade

Gothersgade

Kronprinsessegade

LES ETOILES
ET UNE ROSE

Kongens
Nytorv

KOMMANDANTEN

Kongens

Holbergsgade

Kong Hans

Holmens Kanal

Bremerholm

Østergade

Barsgade

Knippels
bro

Christians Brygge

KONGENS HAVE

Abenrá

Landemærket

Købmagergade

Skindergade

LE PAVÉ

Ved Stranden

Christiansborg

Tøjhusgade

Frederiksholms Kanal

Gammel Strand

Nybrogade

Vindebrogade

KROGS
FISKERESTAURANT

Klareboderne

Gothersgade

Frederiksborggade

Israels
plads

Vendersgade

Nansensgade

Nørre Farimagsgade

ØRSTEDS
PARKEN

LE PROVENCAL

Fiolstræde

Nørregade

Nørre Voldgade

Sankt Peders Stræde

Gammel-
torv

Vestergade

Nytorv

Larsbjørnsstræde

Farvergade

Studiestræde

Vester Voldgade

Nybrogade

Lønggangstræde

Stormgade

Ny Kongensgade

H. C. Andersens Boulevard

Axeltorv

Vesterbrogade

Expensive

ELS Store Strandstræde 3.
❑ 1200-1500, 1730-2200. Bus 1, 6, 9, 10.
Small restaurant specializing in French/Danish cuisine. Beautiful interior.

KONG HANS Vingårdsstræde 6.
❑ 1800-2200 Mon.-Sat. Bus 1, 6, 9, 28, 29, 41.
Reputed to be the best in town. Haute cuisine using the best ingredients.

KROGS FISKERESTAURANT Gammel Strand 38.
❑ 1700-2230. Bus 28, 29, 41.
This restaurant has an extensive fish and seafood menu.

LES ETOILES ET UNE ROSE Dronningens Tværgade 43.
❑ 1200-1400, 1730-2200 Mon.-Fri., 1730-2200 Sat. Bus 10.
The only Danish restaurant with a Michelin star. Excellent service.

LE PAVÉ Gråbrødretorv 14.
❑ 1130-1530, 1730-2200 Mon.-Sat. Bus 5, 28, 29, 41.
French cuisine served in a pretty basement restaurant.

RESTAURANT KANALEN Wildersplads, Strandgade 52.
❑ 1230-2400 Mon.-Sat. (kitchen closed 1530-1730). Bus 2, 8, 9, 31.
*Beautiful setting beside the canal on Christianshavn (see **WALK 2**, **A-Z**).*

LE PROVENCAL Skindergade 20.
❑ 1700-2300 Mon.-Sat. Bus 5.
Tiny restaurant specializing in Provençal and Corsican food and wine.

RESTAURANT NEPTUN Sankt Annæ Plads 16.
❑ 1200-1500, 1800-2200. Bus 1, 6, 9, 10.
The emphasis here is on fish and seafood, served in a pretty interior.

KOMMANDANTEN Ny Adelgade 7.
❑ 1200-1430, 1730-2200 Mon.-Fri., 1730-2200 Sat. Bus 1, 4E, 6, 7E, 9, 10, 17E, 29, 31.
Smart restaurant, distinctive furnishings. Extensive French/Danish menu.

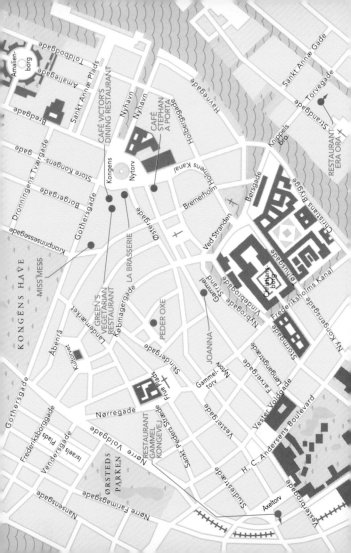

Moderate

JOANNA Læderstræde 11.
❏ 1200-2300 Mon.-Sat. Bus 28, 29, 41.
Small, intimate restaurant, with varied and original international menu.

CAFÉ STEPHAN A PORTA Kongens Nytorv 17.
❏ 1100-2400 Mon.-Sat., 1200-2200 Sun. Bus 1, 6, 9, 10.
Italian restaurant. Glass-covered terrace and turn-of-the-century interior.

MISS MESS Ny Østergade 21.
❏ 1800-2300 Mon.-Sat. Bus 1, 6, 7, 9, 10, 43.
Smart bistro-type restaurant attracting a young, fashionable clientele.

LA BRASSERIE Hotel d'Angleterre, Kongens Nytorv.
❏ 1130-0100 Mon.-Thu., 1130-0200 Fri.-Sat., 1130-2400 Sun.
Bus 1, 6, 9, 10.
Popular French-style bistro. Glass-fronted terrace on Kongens Nytorv.

CAFÉ VICTOR'S DINING RESTAURANT Ny Østergade 8.
❏ 0900-0200 Mon.-Sat. Bus 1, 6, 7, 9, 10, 43.
Small but original menu. Friendly service and attractive surroundings.

PEDER OXE Gråbrødretorv 2.
❏ 1130-2230. Bus 5.
Typical Danish restaurant with traditional food and interior. Always busy.

GREEN'S VEGETARIAN RESTAURANT Grønnegade 12-14.
❏ 1230-2100 Mon.-Sat. Bus 1, 6, 9, 10, 43.
Good vegetarian menu, self-service. Courtyard restaurant in summer.

RESTAURANT GAMMEL KONGEVEJ Gammel Kongevej 86C.
❏ 1200-2400 Mon.-Sat., 1700-2400 Sun. Bus 1, 14.
In the Frederiksberg district. Traditional Danish menu and live music.

RESTAURANT ERA ORA Torvegade 62.
❏ 1800-2400 Mon.-Sat. Bus 2, 8, 9, 31, 37.
Italian restaurant on Christianshavn with an excellent reputation.

RESTAURANTS 3

Inexpensive

SPISEHUSET Rådhusstræde 13 (in _Huset_ complex – see **NIGHTLIFE**).
❏ 1700-2300 Mon.-Sat. Bus 28, 29, 41.
'Attic' restaurant. Good, inexpensive food, in pleasant surroundings.

SABINE'S CAFETERIA Teglegårdsstræde 4.
❏ 0700-0100 Mon.-Fri., 0900-0100 Sat., 1200-0100 Sun. S-train to
Nørreport.
In the university area. Inexpensive meals and snacks, basic decor.

CAFÉ TORVEHALL Kokkenes Torvehall, Østergade 26.
❏ 1100-1730 Mon.-Thu., 1100-1930 Fri., 1000-1430 Sat. Bus 7.
A busy lunchtime and snack restaurant in an up-market 'foodie' arcade.

CAFÉ SMUKKE MARIE Knabrostræde 19.
❏ 1200-2400 Mon.-Sat., 1600-2400 Sun. Bus 5, 28, 29, 41.
Busy, basement pancake place. Wide range of sweet and savoury fillings.

SPISELOPPEN Bådmandsstræde 43 (2nd floor).
❏ 1700-2300 Thu.-Sun. Bus 2, 8, 9, 31, 37.
Excellent food, good prices and friendly service.

RIZ-RAZ Kompagnistræde 20.
❏ 1130-2400. Bus 28, 29, 41.
Offers a large buffet of Mediterranean cuisine. Advisable to book.

JENSENS BØFHUS Kultorvet 15.
❏ 1200-1500, 1700-2300 Mon.-Sat., 1700-2200 Sun. S-train to N/port.
Large, steak restaurant with inexpensive menus and special offers.

KOH-I-NOOR Vesterbrogade.
❏ 1700-0500. Bus 6.
Good Pakistani restaurant with an extensive and inexpensive buffet.

PASTA BASTA Valkendorfsgade 22.
❏ 1130-0500. Bus 4, 5, 28, 29.
Specializes in pasta dishes. Very popular with Copenhageners.

SPISELOPPEN

_____

See **Eating Out**.

NOUVELLE Gammel Strand 34.
❑ 1130-2200 Mon.-Fri., 1730-2200 Sat. Bus 28, 29, 41. ❑ Expensive.
Elegant restaurant overlooking the canal.

KONGENS KÆLDER Gothersgade 87.
❑ 1100-1600 Mon.-Sat. Bus 1, 6, 7, 9, 10. ❑ Expensive.
*Opposite Kongens Have (see PARKS & GARDENS). Popular with business
people.*

L'ASSIETTE Rosengården.
❑ 1100-1600 Mon.-Fri. S-train to Nørreport. ❑ Moderate.
Cosy traditional restaurant close to the University area.

IDA DAVIDSON Store Kongensgade 70.
❑ 1000-1700 Mon.-Fri. Bus 1, 6, 9. ❑ Moderate.
*Family business, established in 1888. Best smørrebrød (see **Food**) in city.*

RIZOTTO Nytorv 5.
❑ 1000-1630 Mon.-Thu., 1000-1700 Fri. Bus 1, 5, 6, 8, 14, 19, 28, 30,
34, 41, 64, 71E. ❑ Moderate.
Bustling city-centre restaurant with an excellent delicatessen.

CAFÉ PETERSBORG Bredgade 76.
❑ 1130-2100 Mon.-Sat. Bus 1, 6, 9. ❑ Inexpensive.
Established in 1746 and renowned for some of the house specialities.

DET LILLE APOTEK Store Kannikestræde 15.
❑ 1100-0200 Mon.-Sat., 1200-2400 Sun. S-train to Nørreport; bus 5.
❑ Inexpensive.
Offers the best of traditional food in a 200-year-old restaurant.

SORGENFRI Brolæggerstræde 8.
❑ 1100-0200 (dinner until 2045). Bus 5, 28, 29, 41. ❑ Inexpensive.
Located in an 18thC building. Once the haunt of fishwives and sailors.

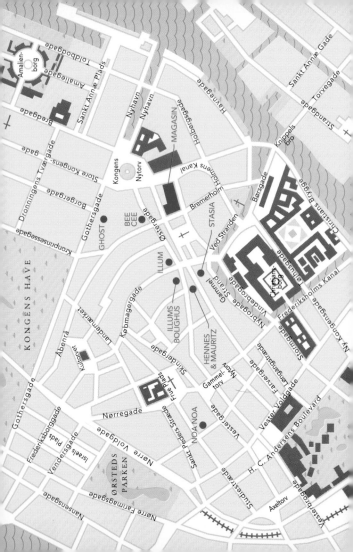

Dept Stores/Fashions

❏ See **Opening Times**.

ILLUM Amagertorv 52.
S-train to Nørreport; bus 1, 2, 5, 6, 8, 10, 15E, 28, 29, 41, 43.
One of the city's two largest stores. Five floors selling fashions, house-hold goods, gifts, etc. Also contains restaurants, a bank and a cinema.

ILLUMS BOLIGHUS Amagertorv 10.
S-train to Nørreport; bus 1, 2, 5, 6, 8, 10, 15E, 28, 29, 41, 43.
Presents the best of modern design in furniture, kitchen-ware, porcelain, glass, etc. Emphasis on Danish and Scandinavian design.

MAGASIN Kongens Nytorv 13.
Bus 1, 6, 9, 10, 15E, 29, 31, 43.
Large department store with a particularly good food hall.

HENNES & MAURITZ Amagertorv 25.
S-train to Nørreport; bus 1, 2, 5, 6, 8, 10, 15E, 28, 29, 41, 43.
Inexpensive fashions, plus children's clothes, shoes and cosmetics.

BEE CEE Østergade 24 (also an entrance in Pistolstræde).
Bus 1, 6, 9, 10, 43.
Exclusive shop selling the creations of the top fashion houses – Chanel, Yves St. Laurent, Kenzo, Ralph Lauren.

STASIA Læderstæde 3.
Bus 1, 2, 5, 6, 8, 10, 15E, 28, 29, 41.
Fashions by Danish designer, Stasia – very distinctive Copenhagen style.

GHOST Grønnegade 27.
Bus 1, 6, 9, 10, 43.
Original and stylish women's fashions in crushed silks and velvets.

NOA NOA Larsbjørnstræde 16 (and other branches around town).
Fashionable leisure clothes for women, in cotton and T-shirt fabrics. Reasonably priced and very much in the Danish style.

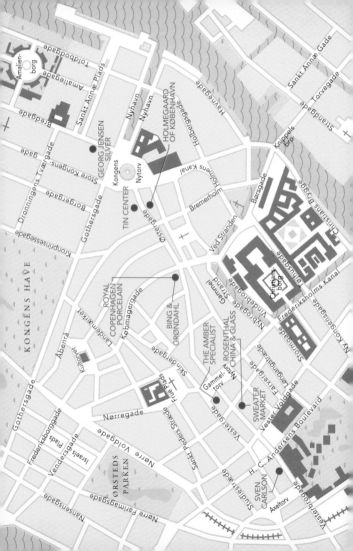

KONGENS HAVE

Amalien-
borg

Toldbodgade

Amaliegade

Sankt Annæ Gade

Sankt Annæ Plads

Bredgade

Bredgade

GEORG JENSEN SILVER

Store Kongensgade

Dronningens Tværgade

Borgergade

Gothersgade

Kronprinsessegade

Nyhavn

Nyhavn

Kongens

Nytorv

Østergade

HOLMEGAARD OF KØBENHAVN

Holbergsgade

Havnegade

Torvegade

Strandgade

Sankt Annæ Gade

TIN CENTER

Bremerholm

Holmens Kanal

Knippels bro

Børsgade

Christians Brygge

Ved Stranden

Gammel Strand

Nybrogade

Vindebrogade

Christians borg

Tøjhusgade

Frederiksholms Kanal

ROYAL COPENHAGEN PORCELAIN

Købmagergade

BING & GRØNDAHL

Skindergade

Landemærket

Kultorv

Abenrå

Ny Kongensgade

Stormgade

Løngangstræde

Nørregade

Fiolstræde

Frue Plads

THE AMBER SPECIALIST

Gammel torv

Nytorv

ROSENTHAL CHINA & GLASS

Farvergade

Vester Voldgade

Gothersgade

Frederiksborggade

Israels Plads

Vendersgade

Nansensgade

Nørregade

Sankt Peders Stræde

Nørre Voldgade

ØRSTEDS PARKEN

Nørre Farimagsgade

Studiestræde

Vestergade

SWEATER MARKET

H. C. Andersens Boulevard

Larslejsstræde

SVEN CARLSON

Axeltorv

Vesterbrogade

Gifts & Souvenirs

❏ See **Opening Times**.

ROYAL COPENHAGEN PORCELAIN Amagertorv 6.
BING & GRØNDAHL Amagertorv 4. Bus 1, 2, 5, 6, 8, 10, 28, 29.
Two shops, set side by side, present the widest possible selection of porcelain – tableware, ornaments, lamps, and many other items.

GEORG JENSEN SILVER Bredgade 411 & Østergade 40.
Bus 1, 6, 9, 10.
Long-established silversmiths. The Bredgade branch sells second-hand silver, the Østergade shop has new silver pieces and modern designs.

ROSENTHAL CHINA AND GLASS Frederiksberggade 21.
S-train to Central Station; bus 1, 6, 8, 14, 16, 28, 41.
World-famous company known for its elegant and distinctive designs.

THE AMBER SPECIALIST Frederiksberggade 2.
S-train to Central Station; bus 1, 6, 8, 14, 16, 28, 41.
A souvenir which is particularly Danish. Jewellery created from amber collected from the beaches around Denmark.

SWEATER MARKET Frederiksberggade 15.
S-train to Central Station; bus 1, 6, 8, 14, 16, 28, 41.
Traditional Scandinavian sweaters, in a wealth of styles and patterns.

HOLMEGAARD OF KØBENHAVN Østergade 15.
Bus 1, 6, 9, 10, 43.
Beautiful creations in glass, with something to suit every pocket.

TIN CENTER Ny Østergade 2.
Pewter is a traditional Danish export, and here one can choose from traditional, reproduction and modern designs.

SVEN CARLSON Vesterbrogade 2B.
Large souvenir shop. Two floors offer every type of souvenir from Copenhagen T-shirts to porcelain and Scandinavian sweaters.

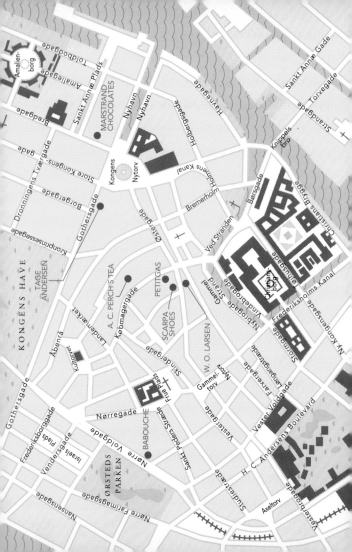

❏ See **Opening Times**.

W. O. LARSEN Amagertorv 9.
S-train to Nørreport; bus 1, 2, 5, 6, 8, 10, 15E, 28, 29, 41, 43.
Pipe and tobacco shop, established 1864. The old original wood pan-elling, shelves, cases and counters are still in place. A Tobacco Museum is at the same address.

SCARPA SHOES Amagertorv. (Enter through courtyard.)
S-train to Nørreport; bus 1, 2, 5, 6, 8, 10, 15E, 28, 29, 41, 43.
One of the best shoe shops in town specializing in modern, stylish footwear for men and women.

MARSTRAND CHOCOLATES Bredgade 14.
Bus 1, 6, 9, 10.
Basement shop selling the most luxurious chocolates in town.

PETITGAS Købmagergade 5.
S-train to Nørreport; bus 1, 2, 5, 6, 8, 10, 15E, 28, 29, 41, 43.
Hats for gentlemen, established 1875. Original interior.

A. C. PERCH'S TEA Kronprinsensgade 5.
S-train to Nørreport; bus 1, 2, 5, 6, 8, 10, 15E, 28, 29, 41, 43.
Established 1835, this tiny shop still boasts the original interior. Perch's specialize exclusively in tea, importing and blending it themselves.

TAGE ANDERSEN Ny Adelgade 12.
Bus 1, 6, 9, 10.
This amazing shop is a must – interior design, flowers and plants.

BABOUCHE Nørre Voldgade 2.
S-train to Nørreport; bus 4E, 14, 16, 74E.
Leather boots and slippers in unusual designs, jackets and hats from Morocco and Guatemala, bags and jewellery. Some of the items are by Danish designers.

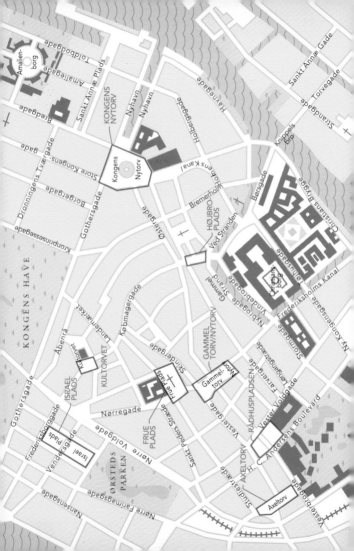

KONGENS NYTORV East end of Østergade.
Bus 1, 4E, 6, 7E, 9, 10, 17E, 29, 31.
Largest square in the city, dominated by the Kongelige Teater. See **A-Z**.

RÅDHUSPLADSEN West end of Strøget.
S-train to Vesterport; bus 1, 6, 8, 14, 19, 28, 30, 34, 41, 64, 71E.
Overlooked by the Town Hall (see **Rådhus**) *on its south side and enhanced by the fairy lights of Tivoli (see* **A-Z**) *in the evening.*

KULTORVET South of Nørreport station.
S-train to Nørreport; bus 4E, 5, 14, 16, 74E.
This lively square is surrounded by cafés, and filled with fruit and flower stalls. Its name comes from the charcoal burners who used to trade here.

GAMMEL TORV/NYTORV On Strøget.
S-train to Vesterport or Central Station; bus 1, 6, 8, 14, 19, 28, 30, 34.
Together these two form one very busy square. Fruit and flower stalls are joined by trinket traders in summer.

HØJBROPLADS East end of Amagertorv.
Bus 1, 2, 5, 6, 8, 10, 15E, 43.
From this square you get one of the best views of Old Copenhagen's main sights. A statue of Bishop Absalon is the main feature. See **WALK 2**.

FRUE PLADS Off Nørregade.
S-train to Nørreport; bus 14, 40, 43, or any to Rådhuspladsen.
Marks the beginning of the university area. Vor Frue Kirke (see **CHURCHES**) *sits in the centre, and the university buildings to the north.*

ISRAEL PLADS North of Nørreport Station.
S-train to Nørreport; bus 14, 40, 43.
Site of a flea-market every Saturday morning (see **Markets**).

AXELTORV Between Palads, Cirkus Bygning and the Scala centre.
S-train to Vesterport or Central Station; bus 1, 2, 6, 12, 13, 16, 28, 41.
A traffic-free square, with many cafés, sculptures and fountains.

TREKRONER

LANGELINIE PROMENADE
(Langelinie)

Østbanegade

Strandboulevarden

Nordre Frihavnsgade

Østerbrogade

Østerbrogade

Classensgade

Gittervej

Sortedams Sø

Øster Farimagsgade

Dag Hammarskjölds Allé

Kristianiagade

ØSTERPORT

Østbanegade

Stockholmsgade

Folke Bernadottes Allé

Grønningen

Store Kongensgade

POLAR BEAR
& CUBS

SØFARTSMONUMEN

Gittervej

NORWEGIAN
GATE

Forbindelsesvej

DEN LILLE HAVFRUE

KASTELLET

LANGELINIE
PAVILLONEN

KING'S
GATE

IRON BRIDGE

GEFION
FOUNTAIN

Espenaden

ST. ALBAN'S
CHURCH

Sølvgade

Rigensgade

Kronprinsessegade

Fredericiagade

Borgergade

Amaliegade

Øster Voldgade

Sølvgade

FRIHEDSMUSEET

KONGENS
HAVE

Store Kongensgade

Bredgade

Toldbodgade

Gothersgade

Sankt Annæ Plads

Købmagergade

Kongens
Nytorv

Østergade

Nyhavn
Nyhavn

Holbergsgade

3hr.

If you don't feel like walking all the way from the centre of town to the beginning of this walk, you can take the train to Østerport station (two stops from Vesterport, one from Nørreport) and proceed from there, heading back towards town from where the walk ends. It is also possible to take a bus back into the town centre from the finishing point. Coming out of Østerport station, turn to the left, cross Folke Bernadottes Allé and enter the park where you see signs for 'Langelinie' and 'Den Lille Havfrue'. This brings you into the park surrounding the Citadel (Kastellet – see **A-Z**). The path brings you down to the moat, from where you should follow it round to the right. It is a pleasant walk around the moat, and you will be able to see the walls of the Citadel, high up on the other side, and also the Old Mill, which sits on the ramparts behind the buildings at the centre of the fort. A ten-minute stroll brings you to the southern entrance of Kastellet, via the King's Gate. Inside, the atmosphere is very much that of a barracks. The two-storied brick buildings known as 'stokken' are lined up in neat rows, and the fortress is still in use by the Danish military.

Leave the Citadel by its northern (Norwegian) gate and cross the street into the park on the right-hand side. You are now on Langelinie (see **PARKS & GARDENS**, **A-Z**). Close to the entrance is the striking Søfartsmonument (see **A-Z**), with its dramatic winged figure. Next to the monument lies the Lystbådehavnen, a small yachting marina. Carry on past the marina to the beginning of the actual Langelinie Promenade. This stretches for about another kilometre. Although you may not want to walk all the way along, do go the short distance to the statue of the polar bear and her cubs, which stands at the edge of Langelinie Quay, just over the bridge. This is also an excellent spot from which to enjoy the view across the Sound. You can see the many small islands which lie between Copenhagen and the Swedish coast. This is a very busy stretch of water, with a continuous stream of speedy hydrofoil ferries shuttling backwards and forwards between Malmö in Sweden and Copenhagen. Farthest out on Langelinie, to the left, can be seen one of the original customs buildings of Frihavnen, built of sandstone in 1894. From here a careful watch could be kept on the movements of all shipping going to and from Frihavnen.

Turn, and start to walk back along the quay. Out to the east lies Trekroner, originally a sea fort, and in the 1930s a popular pleasure resort. A little further on, up on a raised platform, sits a long, two-storied building, Langelinieskuret, built by J. V. Dahlerup in 1894. Here, next to Langelinie Quay, cruise ships and visiting military ships often dock. On the northern pier, by the marina, sits Myllus-Erichsen Monument, a dramatic sculpture in black granite, raised in memory of the men who died in the Denmark Expedition to Greenland in 1906-07.

Continue along Langelinie to see the biggest attraction in Copenhagen – The Little Mermaid (see **A-Z**). Further on you will pass the new Langelinie Pavilion, built in 1957 by Eva and Nils Koppel. The next large monument is J. V. Dahlerup's Ivar Hvitfeldt, commemorating the battle of Køge Bugt against the Swedes in 1710. Cross the Iron Bridge, the earliest of its kind built in Denmark, to the end of Langelinie, marked by the spectacular Gefion Fountain (see **A-Z**). Next to the fountain, at the beginning of Churchillparken, sits the English Church of St. Alban's (see **Religious Services**). Near here also is the bust of Sir Winston Churchill, an unusual portrait with Churchill's head tilted slightly to one side, in a rather quizzical manner. Beyond Churchill, an old grey tank marks the entrance to the Frihedsmuseet, museum of the Danish Resistance movement (see **WALK 4**, **MUSEUMS 1**, **A-Z**). From here you can take a bus from Store Kongensgade, a short walk along Esplanaden, to return to Kongens Nytorv or Rådhuspladsen (see **SQUARES**) – or you may choose to stroll on towards Amaliehaven (see **PARKS & GARDENS**), Amalienborg and Nyhavn (see **A-Z**).

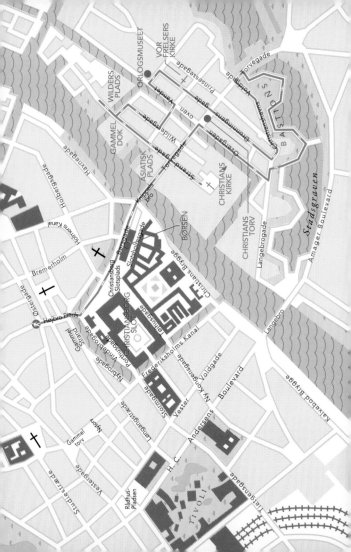

Christianshavn

2hr, excluding visits to museums, churches, etc.

Begin at Højbroplads (see **SQUARES**). Cross onto Slotsholmen, past Christiansborg Slot (see **BUILDINGS**, **A-Z**) and Børsen (see **BUILDINGS**) and walk over Knippelsbro towards Christianshavn. After crossing the bridge, turn right along Strandgade and walk down towards Christians Kirke (built 1755-59 – see **CHURCHES**) which stands at the far end of the street. The short walk along the southern end of Strandgade leads past some of the old merchants' houses on the left-hand side, and on the right lie parts of the old docks and shipbuilding area. Empty buildings here are now being brought to life again, housing art galleries, venues for stage productions, and artists' workshops.

After visiting Christians Kirke, walk back along Strandgade and turn right into Torvegade. Continue until you come to the canal. This part of Copenhagen is reminiscent of Dutch canal towns, and these were, in part, an inspiration for the design and construction of Christianshavn. When Christianshavn was first laid out and built in the mid-17thC, it was a small town separate from Copenhagen – another of Christian IV's creations (see **Christian IV**). The rectilinear layout bears witness to his creed of 'order and efficiency'.

Cross the canal and turn right to walk along Overgaden oven Vandet (the 'street over the water'). The houses lining the street are a strange mixture of shabby and smart. This is now becoming a fashionable area in which to live, and signs of renovation and fresh paintwork are everywhere. When you reach the end of the canal, veer to the left and walk up onto Christianshavns Voldgade. Here you are on the old bastions of the city, and it is still possible to see the structure of the bastions jutting out of the moat. Come down from the bastions, to Dronningensgade. On the left-hand side is Store Søndervoldstæde, where you will find the building which houses the Danish Film Museum (see **A-Z**), Film Institute, and Film School. Halfway along Dronningensgade is Christians Torv, originally the centre of Christianshavn. Here you can see Sven Rathsack's beautiful Greenland sculptures, illustrating the strong links which Christianshavn has always had with that island. Cross Torvegade, and walk further along Dronningensgade, until you reach Vor Frelsers Kirke (see **CHURCHES**, **A-Z**). If you are feeling fit and have a head for heights, a trip to the top of the church's spiral tower

offers a magnificent view of Copenhagen on a clear day. From here, walk back down towards the canal and back onto Overgaden oven Vandet. At No. 58 is the Søkvæsthuset (Naval Hospital), home of the Orlogsmuseet (Naval Museum – see **MUSEUMS 1**). Cross the canal and walk up to Wildersgade, turn right into this street, and continue to the angle of the canal. Turn left along Christianshavn Kanal to the little bridge that crosses over to Wilders Plads. Here you will see some of the yellow-washed houses which remain from the great ship-building era, including a timbered house from 1736 which housed a sailmaker and shipwright. Walk back along Strandgade, past two warehouses from the Florissante Period (1760s), designed by J. C. Conradi. The northernmost of these two buildings has, since 1781, been owned and used by the Royal Greenland Trading Company. Further along Strandgade, on the site of an old Naval Dock (from which its name derives) is Gammel Dok (see **A-Z**), home of the Danish Architecture Centre (see **Arkitektur Center**). Next to Gammel Dok is Asiatisk Plads, lying around one of the man-made harbour basins. The large warehouse to the north was built by Niels Eigtved in 1750. The marble of the facade is from Norway, which was once under Danish rule (1523-1814). All the buildings around Asiatisk Plads now belong to the Foreign Ministry. From Asiatisk Plads walk back onto Knippelsbro, and then across to Slotsholmen to finish the walk.

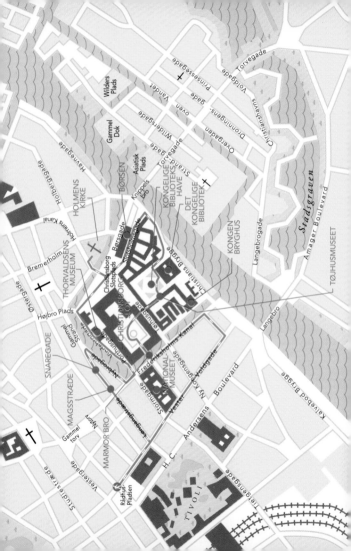

1 hr 30 min, excluding visits to museums, churches, etc.

Start from Rådhuspladsen (see **SQUARES**). Walk southeast down Vester Voldgade towards Christians Brygge. As you approach the harbour you will see evidence of Copenhagen's prosperous sea-trading days in the 18th and 19thC, in the large merchants' buildings and warehouses situated in this area. You will also see some earlier buildings – low, yellow-washed cottages from the 17thC, set in cobbled courtyards.

At Brygghusgade, turn left and walk along to Frederiksholms Kanal. The large brick building on the opposite side of the canal is the old King's Brewery (Kongen Bryghus), built in 1616. Looking along the canal there is a very pleasant view, with 17thC houses lining the canalside, and many boats moored in the water. Further up you can see the Marble Bridge (see **Marmor Bro**) and the palace, Christiansborg Slot (see **BUILDINGS, A-Z**).

Thorvaldsens Museum

Walk along to the Marble Bridge and cross it to come into the Riding Ground of Christiansborg Palace. Ahead is the Palace, and between the Riding Ground and the Palace an equestrian statue of King Christian IX. From here, cross over into Tøjhusgade, to the Tøjhusmuseet (Royal Arsenal Museum – see **MUSEUMS 2**). From the courtyard you can enter the lovely garden of the Royal Library, the Kongelige Biblioteks Have (see **PARKS & GARDENS**). In the garden, shaded by trees, there is a statue of the philosopher Søren Kierkegaard (see **A-Z**) and at

the far end sits the Royal Library (see **BUILDINGS**).

Leave the garden by its south side, coming onto Christians Brygge. Turn left to walk up to Børsgade, which will bring you past the Børsen (see **BUILDINGS**), the Stock Exchange. Before returning to Christiansborg Slotsplads, turn right and cross the canal to see Holmens Kirke (see **CHURCHES**).

Return to Slotsholmen, walk past the front of Christiansborg Palace, with the equestrian statue of Frederik VII standing in front, and you will see the Palace Chapel, sitting separately from the Palace, though joined to it by a passageway. With the canal in front of you, and Gammel Strand just across the water, stay on Slotsholmen and turn left into Vindebrogade, following the canalside until you reach Porthusgade, and are by now walking along the side of the Thorvaldsens Museum (see **MUSEUMS 2, A-Z**). This will give a good opportunity for examining the building's distinctive painted frieze.

From here, walk further along, back to Frederiksholms Kanal. Now cross the canal by the bridge here. Facing you, near the corner of Vestergade, is the entrance to the Nationalmuseet (see **MUSEUMS 1, A-Z**). Turn to the right and cross over into Nybrogade. From here, walking up and away from the canal brings you to the two oldest streets in Copenhagen – Snaregade and Magsstræde – narrow streets whose buildings are twisted and buckled with age. The two oldest houses in the city are located in Magsstræde at Nos 17 and 19. Walk along Løngangstræde, back into Vester Voldgade and return to Rådhuspladsen.

Østerbrogade
Nordre Frihavnsgade
Strandboulevarden
Østbanegade
Gittervej

Østerbrogade
Classensgade

Sortedams Sø

Dag Hammarskjölds Allé
Kristianiagade
Østbanegade
Folke Bernadottes Allé
Gittervej
Forbindelsesvej

Øster Farimagsgade
Stockholmsgade

FRIHEDSMUSEET

NORDRE
TOLDBOD

Grønningen
Store Kongensgade

SANKT
ANSGAR
KIRKE

Esplanaden

Sølvgade

Rigensgade

Øster Voldgade

Frederica gade
Sølvgade
Borgergade

KONGENS
HAVE

KUNSTINDUSTRIMUSEET

Amaliegade

ALEXANDER
NEWSKY KIRKE

Kronprinsessegade
Store Kongensgade

DEHNS
PALÆ

BERNSTORFFS PALÆ

Gothersgade

FREDERIKS
KIRKE

Toldbodgade

AMALIEHAVEN

Bredgade

AMALIENBORG
SLOT

SANKT ANNÆ
PLADS

Købmagergade

Kongens
Nytorv

Bredgade

ODD FELLOW
PALÆ

Østergade

Nyhavn
Nyhavn

GARNISONS
KIRKE

Holbergsgade

Frederiksstaden

2 hr, excluding visits to museums, churches, etc.

Start from Kongens Nytorv (see **SQUARES**) and walk along the north side of Nyhavn (see **A-Z**). Most of the houses in this area date from the 17th and 18thC. At the end of Nyhavn, at No. 71, an early-19thC warehouse has now been converted into a hotel, and near to this building the Fyrskib (Lightship) XVII is moored. From this southernmost point of Frederiksstaden (see **A-Z**) there is an excellent view across the harbour to Christianshavn (see **WALK 2**, **A-Z**) and the 18thC warehouses lining the harbour basin. Walk along Toldbodgade. At No. 24 is the Admiral Hotel, formerly two 18thC grain warehouses. Just beyond lies Amaliehaven (see **PARKS & GARDENS**). From here proceed up to Amalienborg Slot (see **A-Z**). You might want to time the walk so that you arrive here at 1200 noon, in time for the Changing of the Guard. Exit on the north side of Amalienborg and walk along Amaliegade – named after Frederik III's queen, Queen Sophie Amalie. An elegant street, its most noteworthy house is No. 18 – Det Gule Palæ (the Yellow Mansion) which, from the beginning of the 18thC and into the 20thC, was used as a residence by various members of the royal family. Since 1883, the building has been occupied by the Lord Chamberlain's department.

On reaching Esplanaden, turn right and walk down towards Nordre Toldbod. As you walk along Esplanaden, Churchillparken is on the left-hand side. On the way to the Toldbod you also pass the low wooden building which houses the Frihedsmuseet (see **WALK 1**, **MUSEUMS 1**, **A-Z**). At Nordre Toldbod sit the two reception Pavilions between which a red carpet is laid when members of the royal family, or honoured guests of the city, alight here. If you have the time and energy you may want to continue a little further along the quayside for a look at some of the 18thC warehouses standing along the water's edge.

Return along Esplanaden to Bredgade – an elegant street, which even today echoes the 'grand design' of Frederiksstaden. It is a wide, straight avenue, lined with a series of impressive buildings, classical in line and proportion. Bredgade contains many buildings of particular interest. The first of these, at No. 68, is the Kunstindustrimuseet (see **MUSEUMS 1**) and just beyond it at No. 64 sits Sankt Ansgar Kirke (see **CHURCHES**) with the Museum of Medical History further along at No. 62.

A striking feature in Bredgade are the three gold onion domes of Alexander Newsky Kirke at No. 53 (see **CHURCHES**). Just beyond Alexander Newsky Kirke and opposite Frederiksgade, Bredgade opens out to the right and here sits Frederiks Kirke, also known as the Marble Church (see **Marmor Kirke**). Opposite Frederiks Kirke, on the corners of Bredgade and Frederiksgade, sit the twin mansions of Bernstorffs Palæ and Dehns Palæ, built exactly alike in the middle of the 18thC, based on designs by Nicolai Eigtved. Further still along Bredgade, and set back slightly from the street, is Odd Fellow Palæ – originally built for the Berckantin family in 1751, then owned by the Schimmelmann family during whose time it became known for the artistic and literary salons which were held here. In 1984 it became a concert hall. Next on the left is Sankt Annæ Plads, an elegant square, with trees and flower beds laid out in the centre, and an equestrian statue of Christian X facing towards Bredgade. On the right-hand side of Sankt Annæ Plads is Garnisons Kirke, a church built in 1703-06. Walk back onto Bredgade, past the auction showrooms and exclusive antique shops which occupy this section of the street, and return to Kongens Nytorv.

Botanic Gardens palm hou

Royal Library gardens

Accidents & Breakdowns: Under Danish law, in the event of any motor accident, no matter how slight, you must stop, and you must provide your name, address, insurance-company details and car-registration number to others involved. It is not always necessary to contact the police. However, in a more serious accident – involving injuries to people, or where, for example, someone under the influence of alcohol is involved – the police must be contacted. There are telephones on motorways, for use in the event of an accident or breakdown. Falck Redningskorps offer a 24-hr breakdown service. Their telephone numbers vary depending on the area, but can be found in Danish telephone directories. See **Consulates**, **Driving**, **Emergency Number**, **Police**.

Accommodation: Most of the accommodation in Copenhagen is in hotels, classed as luxury, medium and budget class (with or without bath). The majority of hotels are situated close to the city centre, with a large concentration on the west side of Rådhuspladsen (see **SQUARES**) in the Vesterbro area. In the hotels at the top end of the price range, you can enjoy first-class restaurants, leisure-club or gym facilities, in some cases swimming pools – and a high level of comfort and service. Even in the less expensive hotels, you can expect to find the basic comforts, including television and tea- or coffee-making facilities in the rooms. All hotels offer the facility of a third bed in a double room, for a small extra charge. As a rough guide, you can expect to pay 1300-2500kr plus (luxury), 950-1200kr (medium) and 630-950kr (reasonable) for a double room, with bath or shower, and with breakfast included. Danish State Railways and Scandinavian Airlines System (SAS) have special deals with some hotels and it is worth checking on these. It is also worth checking with hotels or with travel agents, since many hotels offer special weekend, or off-season rates, and also special group rates. There is a Room Service kiosk in Central Station (see **Hovedbanegård**) which is open 0900-1700 Mon.-Sat. (1-30 April); 0900-2400 Mon.-Fri., 0900-1400 Sat., 0900-1300 Sun. & hol. (1 May-31 Aug.); 0900-1700 Mon.-Fri., 0900-1200 Sat. (1 Sep.-1 Mar.). You give details of the type of accommodation required (price, etc.) on a form and pay a small fee for the service. Danvisit, H. C. Andersens Boulevard 22, also offers a room-finding service. They are open the same hours as the Tourist

Information office except in July and August when the hours are 0900-2000 Mon.-Fri., 0900-1700 Sat., Sun. See **Camping**, **Tourist Information**, **Youth Hostels**.

Airport: Copenhagen's large, international and very modern airport is located 7 km south of the city at Kastrup on the island of Amager (see **A-Z**). It has excellent facilities including a bank with extended opening hours (see **Money**), various shops and restaurants, public toilets, a left-luggage office and public telephones. There are buses which run to the city centre and a taxi rank outside. All major international airlines have offices here and the main car-rental companies operate from the airport (see **Car Hire**). For flight information contact: British Airways, tel: 33146000; Aer Lingus, tel: 33126055; Canadian Airlines International, tel: 33129523; Pan Am, tel: 33151477; TWA, tel: 31501360; SAS, tel: 31541701.

Amager: An island which lies to the east of Copenhagen city centre and stretching south. Christianshavn (see **A-Z**) is located on Amager, just across the harbour channel, over Langebro and Knippelsbro. The airport (see **A-Z**) is further south on the island and Dragør lies down in the southeast corner. See **EXCURSION 4**.

Amalienborg Slot: The Danish royal family's Copenhagen residence, and setting for the Changing of the Guard. This takes place every day at 1200 and if the Queen or Prince Regent is in residence, is accompanied by music. The Royal Life Guards parade at 1130 in Rosenborg Slot (see **A-Z**) and proceed along the streets towards Amalienborg, passing through Kongens Nytorv (see **SQUARES**), Bredgade and Amaliegade. After the changing of the guard, the return march is made to Rosenborg. Amalienborg was one of the key elements in the design of Frederiksstaden (see **WALK 4**, **A-Z**). Four identical mansions surround a fine square, at the centre of which is an equestrian statue of King Frederik V. The mansions were originally owned and occupied by four prominent aristocratic families, but after the destruction of Christiansborg Slot (see **A-Z**) by fire in 1794, the royal family gradually bought over all of the houses. See **BUILDINGS**, **WALK 4**.

Andersen, Hans Christian (1805-75): Famous for children's fairy tales – *The Little Mermaid* (see **A-Z**), *The Ugly Duckling*, *The Princess and the Pea*, etc. – he was born the son of a shoemaker in Odense, on the island of Fyn. He moved to Copenhagen at the age of 14 and joined Kongelige Teater (see **A-Z**) with hopes of becoming an actor or a dancer. The theatre's director helped him to enter grammar school, first in the town of Slagelse, and later in Helsingør (see **EXCURSION 2, A-Z**). He graduated in 1828, and in 1831 he began on the first of many journeys abroad. When in Copenhagen, he lived in Nyhavn (see **A-Z**) at No. 67 and later at No. 18. Although he wrote novels for adults it was in his children's stories that he found his element.

Arkitektur Center: Situated on Christianshavn (see **WALK 2, A-Z**) and housed in Gammel Dok (see **A-Z**), a restored 18thC warehouse, the Danish Architecture Centre contains a conference centre, an exhibition area, a small bookshop and a pleasant restaurant, with excellent views of the canal and harbour areas. See **WALK 2**.

Assistens Kirkegård: This large churchyard (entrance on Kapelvej) contains the burial places of H. C. Andersen (see **A-Z**) and Søren Kierkegaard (see **A-Z**). S-train to Nørreport; bus 5, 7, 16,18.

Baby-sitters: For child-care services in the city try: Personal Agency, Nørregade 53, tel: 31324019 (0900-2000); Studenternes Babysitters, Smallegade 52A, tel: 31190090 (0700-2100 Mon.-Thu., 1500-1800 Fri., 1500-1700 Sat.). Baby-sitting rates are approx. 25kr per hour (minimum period, 6 hr – daytime, 3 hr – evening) with an additional booking fee of 25kr. See **CHILDREN**.

Bakken: See **EXCURSION 1**.

Banks: See **Currency, Money, Opening Times**.

Best Buys: Danish design is world renowned, with a reputation for simplicity combined with practicality. If you want souvenirs which are typically and exclusively Danish, there is no doubt that a piece of

Danish glass or porcelain is a good idea – and the range has something for every taste and pocket. Denmark is also famous for its silver, gold, and pewterwork. Some of the most outstanding and practical of Danish modern design has been created in stainless steel – look out for the products of a company called Form and Function which has produced the most basic of household objects, e.g. a can opener or paper knife, in the simplest and most beautiful of designs. Another example of good Danish design are children's toys, such as Lego and Duplo. Handmade bone utensils are exclusive to Denmark, as is the beautiful amber jewellery made from pieces washed up on the beaches around the country. Practical presents from the cold north include warm, brightly patterned Scandinavian sweaters, and the lightest and warmest of duvets. For smokers, Copenhagen can be a paradise. The Danish take their smoking very seriously and there are scores of specialist shops selling pipes, tobacco and cigars. If you are interested in antiquarian books the two best areas for browsing are in Gammel Kongevej in the Frederiksberg area of the city, and around the university area. Copenhagen is an excellent place to find original and unusual designs in leather goods, often at reasonable prices. See **SHOPPING**, **Markets**, **Scala**, **Shopping**.

Bicycle Hire: Personal identification (such as a passport) may be required when hiring a bicycle. Some places to try in the city are: Andersens Cykeludlejning, Møllegade 3, tel: 31391154; Cykeltanken, Godthåbsvej 247, tel: 31871423; Københavns Cykelbørs, Gothersgade 157-159, tel: 31140717. Hire normally costs between 25-50kr per day, plus a deposit of 100-200kr. Bicycles can also be hired at railway stations in North Zealand at Elsinore, Hillerød, Klampenborg and Lyngby from 1 April-31 Oct., tel: 33141701.

Blixen, Karen (1885-1962): A Danish author, famous for her novels and short stories. Among the best-known are *Out of Africa* and *Babette's Feast*, both made into award-winning films. She lived in Kenya from 1914-31 and wrote under the pseudonym of Isak Dinesen. The later part of her life was spent at Rungsted Lund (see **EXCURSION 1**) and at her request the park, in which she is now buried, was made into a bird sanctuary after her death.

Børsen: See **BUILDINGS, WALKS 2 & 3**.

Budget:

Hotel breakfast	varies from 25-98kr
Sandwich (various)	20-25kr
Smørrebrød in a bar	28kr (3 pieces)
Dish of the day	70kr; 45-50kr in small restaurants
Pølser	7-17.50kr, depends on sausage, garnish, etc.
Tea and coffee	10-15kr, some places 20kr, but unlimited supply
Fruit juice (litre)	12.95kr

Beer	approx. 17-18kr (bottle), 25kr (half litre)
Wine (from a shop)	approx. 35kr, good bottle from 55kr upwards
Wine (in a restaurant)	100kr-400/500kr
Cinema tickets	45kr (check newspapers for special offers)

Buses: Copenhagen's HT-buses are single decker, white and mustard-yellow. On the front, above the windscreen, a sign shows the number and the destination. The number is also on the back of the bus. If the bus number is followed by an 'E' this means it is an express bus. Have your money or ticket ready when boarding. If buying a ticket, give your money to the driver; if you have a *Rabatkort* (see **Transport**) you will have to 'clip' this in the small machine just in front of the driver's cabin. Anyone without a valid ticket, or without a clipped ticket, is liable to pay a fine. You always enter by the front entrance, and exit by the middle or rear entrances. There are push buttons to ring a bell when you want to alight. The first buses start at around 0500 (0600 Sun.) with the last buses at around 0030 after which a late-bus service operates between Rådhuspladsen (see **SQUARES**) and towns outside of Copenhagen centre. Most bus drivers can speak some English, should you need help, and you can be sure that there will always be others on the bus who can speak English and will be glad to offer help and directions. Bus stops are also painted white and yellow – they indicate clearly which buses stop there and also have an easily understood sign giving routes and timetables. As the centre of the city has many pedestrian ways, the bus numbers given in this book will take you to the nearest point for any destination in the centre, not necessarily to the exact street. For further information on buses, tel: 31951701. See **Copenhagen Card**, **Transport**.

Cameras & Photography: All the major brands of colour, black-and-white and slide film are available in photography shops, and there are developing and printing establishments all over the city. A 24-hr service for developing and printing is almost universal, and there are scores of kiosks and shops offering a 1-hr service. A roll of film (36 exposures) will cost approx. 49.50kr while the developing and printing will cost approx. 165.50kr. In general there is no problem about taking photographs in museums, etc., but there are variations in what is allowed and in some museums the use of a tripod or flash is forbidden. In churches there is also no problem, except during services, and flash and tripods seem to be generally acceptable.

Camping: Camp sites near the city are always busy so it is advisable to book in advance. You will need a camping carnet or an international camping carnet before you can camp at any of the official sites in Denmark. The international camping carnet cannot be bought in Denmark – you must buy it in your own country. The Danish camping carnet can be bought at all camp sites in Denmark and it is valid for one year (family 48kr, single person 24kr, group – up to 15 persons – 96kr). The cost of an overnight stay at a camp site is approx. 30-35kr per person, half-price for children. Some sites near the city are: Absalon Camping, Korsdalsvej, 2610 Rødovre, tel: 31410600 (open all year); Bellahøj Camping, Hvidkildevej, København NV, tel: 31101150 (open 31 Mar.-1 Oct.); Strandmøllen Camping, Strandvejen, Klampenborg, tel: 42801983 (open 15 May-31 Aug.). A booklet, *Camping Denmark*, which lists all the approved camp sites in the country, can be obtained free from bookshops, or from Friluftsrådet, Skjoldsgade 10, 2100 København Ø, tel: 31423222. For more general information on camping, write or telephone Campingrådet, Olof Palmesgade 10, København 2100 Ø, tel: 31423222. No personal visits.

Car Hire: To be eligible to hire a car in Denmark you must be over 20 years of age and possess a valid driving licence. Individual hire companies may set even higher age limits for renting cars. All the major hire companies have offices in the city: Europcar, Gammel Kongevej 70, tel: 31246677; Avis, Kampmannsgade 1, tel: 31152299; Hertz, Ved Vesterport 3, tel: 31144222; Budget, Nyropsgade 6, tel: 33133900; Inter-Rent, Jernbanegade 6, tel: 31116200; Pitzner, Trommesalen 4, tel: 31111234. They are also represented at the airport (see **A-Z**). All car-hire companies will have different payment schemes depending on the rental period and distance travelled, but, as a simple guide, a typical 'all-inclusive' price with unlimited travel and insurance cover, would be 300kr per day, and 1500kr per week. See **Driving**.

Carlsberg Brewery & Museum: There are organized tours of this large brewery complex at Valby Langgade 1 (tel: 31211221), showing the brewing process and giving information on the history of brewer Jacobsen and his family. The tour begins from the Elephant Gate, the entrance to the brewery (1130 & 1430 Mon.-Fri., or by special arrangement for groups), and includes a visit to the Carlsberg Museum. Bus 6,18; free.

Charlottenborg Slot: The oldest house on Kongens Nytorv (see SQUARES), this baroque building was the residence of Queen Charlotte Amalie and is now the home of the Royal Danish Academy of Art with an exhibition centre at the rear of the palace.

Chemists: Danish chemists are strictly dispensing chemists. They can be identified by the traditional sign of a staff entwined with a serpent or the pestle and mortar. Normal opening hours are 0900-1730 (some open till 1900 on Fri.), 0900-1300 Sat. There are 24-hr chemists at: Steno Apotek, Vesterbrogade 6C, tel: 33148266 and Sønderbro Apotek, Amagerbrogade 158, tel: 31580140. The following are also open 0900-2000 Mon.-Fri., 0900-1730 Sat., 1000-1730 Sun. & hol.: Gothåb Apotek, Gothåbsvej 4; Rødovre Apotek, Roskildevej 258; Trekroner Apotek, Ulgerslev Allé 38. See **Health**.

Children: See CHILDREN, **Baby-sitters**.

Christian IV (1577-1648): During his reign as king (1588-1648) he worked energetically to turn Denmark into northern Europe's biggest power politically, militarily and economically, concentrating especially on building up the country's sea-power. He was also the 'Builder King', and was responsible for many of Copenhagen's fine buildings including the Børsen (see BUILDINGS), Holmens Kirke (see CHURCHES), Rosenborg Slot (see **A-Z**), Trinitatis Kirke with Rundetårn (see **A-Z**) and part of Nyboder, and he planned Christianshavn (see WALK 2, **A-Z**).

Christiania: An independent community lying between Christianshavn (see **A-Z**) and Christians Vold. This 'Free State' began as a social experiment in the early 1970s, after being the scene of a giant 'squat' in 1971. Its status was formalized in 1973, with an agreement that the experiment should run for three years. It has been there ever since. The community acknowledges no allegiances to the governing bodies of Copenhagen or of Denmark, and pays no taxes to the state purse. The residents do, however, pay the government each year for electricity. The community has its own 'community purse' into which all residents pay a share, and from which funding is made for the services which Christiania provides for its members, e.g. kindergarten, health care, legal aid, etc. Within Christiania there are shops, cafés and restaurants. The area has a reputation for providing easy access to drugs, and you may be approached openly within the confines of the community. Remember, however, that the possession of drugs is an offence under Danish law (see **Drugs**).

Christiansborg Slot: Christiansborg Palace sits on Slotsholmen (Castle Island). The present building is the fifth to stand on this site. Two previous Christiansborg Palaces were destroyed by fire, one in 1794 and the other in 1884. Still remaining from 18thC Christiansborg are the Riding Ground, lying between the Palace and the Marble Bridge (see **Marmor Bro**), and the two wings which flank it, one of these now containing the Theatre Museum (see MUSEUMS 2) and the Carriage Museum (see **Karetmuseet**). The present baroque palace was built in 1907-28. There are three main parts of the palace which can be visited. The Royal Reception Rooms are a

series of grand apartments used on state occasions and for the Queen's public audiences. There are conducted tours in English at 1100 & 1300 Tue.-Fri., Sun. (Oct.-April); 1100, 1300 & 1500 Tue.-Sun. (May-Sep.); 20kr, child 10kr. The Folketing is the Chambers of the Danish Parliament and there are tours every hour 1000-1600 Sun.-Fri. (June-Sep.), Sun. only (Oct.-May); free. The Palace Ruins are underneath Christiansborg, and excavations have revealed traces of Bishop Absalon's 12thC castle, as well as some traces of the first Christiansborg Palace. The ruins are open 0930-1530 (May-Sep.), 0930-1530 Sun.-Fri. (Oct.-April); 10kr, child 5kr. See **BUILDINGS**, **WALK 3**.

Christianshavn: This area lies on the island of Amager (see **A-Z**). It was originally a separate town from Copenhagen, laid out by Christian IV (see **A-Z**) as a residential and trading centre for the merchants and shipbuilders of the 17thC. See **WALK 2**.

Circus: From June-Oct. you can visit the circular Cirkus Bygning, home of the largest indoor circus in Europe, the Cirkus Benneweis. This family-run circus is now 100 years old. The building also hosts many famous international circuses. See **CHILDREN**, **Copenhagen Card**.

Climate: Generally, not unlike the south of England, but it can be warmer in summer (average temp. 12-18°C) and most certainly will be colder in winter (average temp. 0-5°C). Although it is drier than many parts of the British Isles, it can and does rain, in all seasons. Copenhagen can also be a very windy city. Even in summer it is probably wise to bring a warm sweater, a light jacket or a raincoat. In the winter, warm clothes are needed, along with weatherproof shoes and warm headgear. If that paints a depressing picture, don't worry, because this part of Denmark is also favoured with long spells of clear, bright weather, at all times of year.

Complaints: Tourists with complaints about accommodation, service or any problem connected with their holiday should obtain a complaints form from Tourist Information (see **A-Z**) and return it, completed, to the same office, for the complaint to be examined.

Consulates:

UK – Kastelsvej 36-40, 2100 København Ø, tel: 31264600.
Rep. of Ireland – Østbanegade 21, 2100 København Ø, tel: 31423233.
Australia – Kristianiagade 21, 2100 København Ø, tel: 31262244.
Canada – Kristen Bernikowsgade 1, 1175 København K, tel: 33122299.
USA – Dag Hammersjkolde Allé, 2100 København Ø, tel: 31423144.

Conversion Chart:

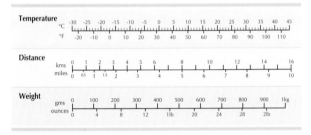

Copenhagen Card: This is well worth buying if you are going to be in the city for a few days and want to see as much as possible, in the least expensive fashion. The card is issued by the Copenhagen Tourist Association and is available to all tourists. It can be bought at all main railway stations, at Danvisit and the Tourist Information office (see **Tourist Information**), hotels and travel agencies. It entitles the bearer to free and unlimited travel on buses and trains in the central Copenhagen area (see **Transport**), 25% or 50% discount on ferry fares to and from Sweden, free admission to all the main museums and sights including Tivoli (see **A-Z**) and 25% discount on Circus tickets (see **Circus**). The card is valid for between one and three days and costs 90kr, 140kr, or 180kr, depending on the duration of usage, half price for children under 12. An explanatory brochure, in English, is also available with the card.

Credit Cards: See **Money**.

Crime & Theft: As in any big city, Copenhagen has its share of pick-pockets and car thieves. Common sense dictates many of the rules. Don't leave an obvious holiday-makers' car, filled with all the usual luggage and valuables such as cameras, radios, etc., unattended in the city centre. Some thieves operate only in the area around Tivoli because the pickings are so easy and so rich. There is a left-luggage office and left-luggage lockers at Central Station, Vesterbrogade, where your belongings will be secure. Don't keep all your valuables in one place – try to separate them into different pockets or bags. Any valuables which are not needed constantly can be put into your hotel safe. If you are the victim of a theft, contact the nearest police station. Details of insurance will be requested and details of the stolen items, e.g. credit card numbers. It is advisable to carry a separate note of traveller's cheques numbers, serial numbers of cameras, personal stereos, etc. See **Consulates**, **Emergency Number**, **Insurance**, **Police**.

Currency: The Danish kroner (kr), also known abroad as Dkr, is made up of 100 øre. Notes: 5000, 1000, 500, 100, 50, 20kr; coins: 10, 5, 1kr, and 50 and 25 øre. See **Money**.

Customs Allowances:

Duty Paid Into:	Cigarettes	or	Cigars	or	Tobacco	Spirits	Wine
EC	300		75		400 g	1.5 l	5 l
UK	300		75		400 g	1.5 l	5 l

Danish Film Museum: Part of the Danish Film Institute on Store Søndervoldstræde, it contains a library of film stills, books on films and film makers (1200-1600 Mon.-Fri., also 1830-2100 Tue., Thu.). Films are shown from Sep.-May. See **WALK 2**.

Dentists: See **Health**.

Disabled People: The Tourist Information office (see **Tourist Information**) supplies an excellent free brochure, *Access in Denmark – a Guide for the Disabled*. This gives practical information on all aspects of a holiday which has to cater for the needs of a disabled person – hospitals, medicine, doctors, etc. – as well as telling you where wheelchairs can be hired, advice on transport in Denmark and providing a listing of hotels, restaurants, museums and theatres which have facilities for disabled people. See **Health**.

Doctors: See **Health**.

Domhuset: This neoclassical building on Nytorv (see **SQUARES**), formerly the Town Hall, is now the city court house. It is open to the public 0800-1600 Mon.-Fri.

Domkirke: See **CHURCHES**, **Vor Frue Kirke**.

Drinks: Beer is the national drink and very much part of Danish life. The two favourite brands are those brewed by Carlsberg (see **A-Z**) and Tuborg (see **A-Z**). Gammel Dansk is a strong and bitter-tasting spirit which is definately an acquired taste. The Danes' other spirit is *akvavit* (schnapps), a clear and fiery drink made from potatoes. Wine (*vin*) is very expensive in restaurants, but by the glass in cafés it is reasonably priced although you can never be sure how good it will be. Coffee (*kaffe*) is served strong and black, with milk and sugar separate. Espresso and cappucino are also available. Tea (*te*) is also served black, with milk and sugar provided alongside. Tea with lemon is *te med citron*. If you want mineral water, ask for *mineralvand* or *Danskvand*. Lemonade is *sodavand*.

Driving: In Denmark there is an excellent system of roads and motor-ways, all in good condition, well signposted, and clearly numbered. When driving, the driver and the front-seat passenger must wear seat belts. Driving is on the right and speed limits are 50 kph in built-up areas, 80 kph on highways, 100 kph on motorways and 70 kph for cars with trailer caravans. The only requirement when visiting for a short period is a current driving licence and evidence of proper insurance cover. Denmark has strict drink-driving laws and heavy fines and imprisonment can be imposed if you are found to be driving with over the legal limit of alcohol in your blood. Copenhagen has many one-way streets and pedestrian ways so care is needed if driving in the city. You will also have to get used to the thousands of cyclists. There are cycle paths next to many main roads and streets, but not all, so always be aware of cyclists coming up on the inside. A hazard you might not have expected is roller skaters who seem to use the road like cyclists – watch out for them. The FDM (Federation of Danish Motorists), Firskovvej 32, Lyngby, tel: 45930800, has reciprocal arrangements with the RAC and AA but bring your membership card. They are open 0900-1700 Mon.-Fri. See **Accidents & Breakdowns**, **Car Hire**, **Parking**, **Petrol**, **Transport**.

Drugs: All drugs are illegal in Denmark and there are severe penalties for offenders.

Eating Out: Copenhagen has a reputation for being a very expensive city in which to eat out, and as far as the top restaurants in town are concerned, this is unfortunately very true. It is, however, possible to have a good meal in a restaurant without breaking the bank. Over the past few years Copenhagen has seen a large number of ethnic restaurants open, many serving food at reasonable prices and many offering a *ta-selv bord* (self-service buffet) where you can eat as much as you want for a fixed price. Some of the more expensive Danish/French restaurants also have special offers – often mid-week, and all offer set menus at prices which compare well to the à la carte dishes. In

Copenhagen you will also come across *frokost* restaurants. These very Danish restaurants are normally only open at lunchtime and serve typical Danish cuisine, including smørrebrød, at reasonable prices (see **RESTAURANTS 4**). In all cases, menu details are always displayed outside restaurants. Look out for *Dagens Menu* or *Dagens Ret* signs advertising the inexpensive dish or menu of the day. The *Danmenu* sign means that a restaurant provides good traditional Danish food (two courses) for a fixed price. As a rough guide, a meal for two with drinks will cost as follows: expensive – 900-1200kr; moderate – 400-600kr; inexpensive – approx. 200kr. In cafés it is possible to have just one course for 20-50kr. See **RESTAURANTS**, **Food**, **What's On**.

Electricity: 220 volts AC. Small, continental-style, two-pin plugs are used, so visitors from the UK will need an adaptor.

Emergency Number: Tel: 000 for an ambulance, the fire brigade or police. The number automatically connects with the ambulance and fire service and if the police (see **A-Z**) are required then Falck (the company which handles the other services) will contact them for you.

Events:
1 May: May Day, the traditional workers' day, celebrated with speeches, music, trade-union marches, etc.
End of May/early June: Carnival, this is held at Whitsun (*Pinse*) weekend. On the Saturday there is a large procession through the city and over the whole weekend the city is full of music and dancing.
Sat. in August: Nyhavn festival, a day of music, parades, games, and much more. See **Nyhavn**.
In addition, there are many music festivals which take place all over the city, all year round. For details of these and the other events mentioned above, contact Tourist Information (see **A-Z**) or the Danish Music Information Centre (see **Music**). See **What's On**.

Fishwife Statue: This stands beside the canal on Gammel Strand, marking the spot where all the fishwives used to have their stalls. There is only one left now, and she sets up her stall beside the statue.

FOO

Food: The best-known Danish food is, of course, smørrebrød. These open sandwiches with a base of dark rye bread, can be topped by many combinations of every imaginable ingredient – choose from fish, meat, eggs, vegetables and salad ingredients, with various seasonings and dressings. As well as being able to enjoy the delights of smørrebrød in any *frokost* restaurant (see **Eating Out**) or other restaurants advertising traditional Danish food, you can also 'take away' from the many smørrebrød shops around town. If you want to sam-

ple other traditional Danish dishes, look for: *stegt ål* – eel fried in egg and breadcrumbs; *biksemad* – a fried hash, containing meat, onions, potatoes, often topped with a fried egg; *frikadeller* – meat balls, usually made from a mixture of minced veal and pork, with onion, egg and seasonings; *rødkål* – red cabbage braised with apple and redcurrant jelly; *gulerter* – a filling yellow-pea soup which also contains meat and sausage; *stegte rødspætter* – fried plaice or sole; *leverpostej* – liver paté; *pølser* – hot-dogs, sold from the many stands in the city. *Konditori* are where you can try the wonderful, mouth-watering cakes and pastries the Danes enjoy, such as *lagkage* – a layer cake or gateau and *Wienerbrød* – Danish pastries. See **RESTAURANTS**, **Eating Out**.

Frederiksberg Slot: An elegant Italianate palace built in the early 18thC as a royal summer residence. It is painted in the traditional pale yellow and white and overlooks both Frederiksberg Have and Søndermarken, originally laid out as the palace gardens (see **PARKS & GARDENS**). The main entrance is on Roskildevej. The palace is now a military academy and public access is not allowed but special arrangements can be made for group visits by appointment (tel: 31162244).

Frederiksberg Have

Frederiks Kirke: See **Marmor Kirke.**

Frederiksstaden: This area was designed in the 18thC, at the request of Frederick V, by Nicolai Eigtved, as an extension of the old city. It was made up of fine mansion and town houses, to be occupied by the noble and wealthy families of Copenhagen, with Amalienborg as the heart of the area. See **WALK 4.**

Frihedsmuseet: Set up in memory of the Danish Resistance Movement during the Nazi occupation, the museum pictures daily life in Denmark at that time through photographs, newspapers, uniforms and evidence from concentration camps. See **MUSEUMS 1, WALKS 1 & 4.**

Fyrskib XVII: See **WALK 4.**

Gammel Dok: This renovated 18thC warehouse sits on the dockside in Christianshavn (see **A-Z**). It houses the Arkitektur Center (see **A-Z**), the Danish Arts and Crafts Workshops and the Danish Export Building Council. See **WALK 2.**

Gefion Fountain: A dramatic fountain which sits next to Churchillparken (see **PARKS & GARDENS**, **WALKS 1 & 4**) and St. Alban's Church at the south end of Langelinie (see **A-Z**). It depicts the goddess Gefion, with her four sons transformed into four huge oxen. Legend says that in this manner the goddess ploughed out a huge piece of Sweden, which thereafter became Zealand. See **WALK 1**.

Georg Jensen Silver Museum: This tiny museum inside Jensen's Bredgade shop (see **SHOPPING 2**) displays examples of the fine silver designed by Jensen's since 1904.

Grundtvigs Kirke: This striking church was built as a monument to preacher, Nicholai F. S. Grundtvig (1783-1872), the poet and priest who wrote 1500 psalms. His belief in a 'school for life' led to the setting up of the Folk High Schools in Denmark. Grundtvigs Kirke, which is situated on Bispebjerg, was built between 1921-40 and is typically Danish in its stunningly simple design. Bus 16, 19.

Health: All visitors to Denmark are entitled to free emergency hospital treatment provided they have not come to Demark to receive treatment. Kommunhospitalet, Øster Farimagsgade 5 and Rigshospitalet, Blegdamsvej 9 provide 24-hr emergency treatment. The emergency number for a doctor is 0041. The doctor must be paid at the time of the visit, probably 100-300kr. All Danish doctors use English a great deal in their work and communication with GPs and hospital doctors should be easy. For dental emergency service contact: Tandlægevagten, Oslo Plads 14, near Østerport Station (0800-2130 Mon.-Fri., 1000-1200 Sat., Sun., & hol.). Dentists must also be paid in cash at the time of treatment. Visitors from EC countries have the same rights to treatment as Danish residents and the costs of doctor's, dentist's and chemist's bills will be partly refunded. British citizens would be required to show their passports. The refunds are available at the nearest Health Insurance office (Tourist Information offices – see **A-Z** – have addresses). Refunds should be claimed before you leave, but if you are unable to do so contact the relevant authority when you return home. See **Chemists**, **Disabled People**, **Emergency Number**, **Insurance**.

Helligåndskirke: The Church of the Holy Ghost, situated on Amagertorv, is the oldest church in Copenhagen. Dating originally from c.1400, it was rebuilt in neo-Renaissance style after being damaged by fire in the 18thC.

Helsingør: 59 km north of Copenhagen. Pop: 56,000. Train to Helsingør. Situated on the coast, at the head of Øresund, this town has several interesting sights, including the Teknisk Museum, Marienlyst Castle, Sankt Olaf's Kirke, Sankt Maria Kirke, and nearby Kronborg Castle. See EXCURSION 2.

Hillerød: See EXCURSION 2.

Hirschsprungs Samlingen (Hirschsprung Collection): Housed in a neoclassical building specially designed for the collection by H. P. Storck, this is the best introduction to 19thC Danish art, and particularly to the works of the 'Golden Age' artists. Most of these artists used ordinary Danish people as their subjects, and the paintings also give some insight into the Danish way of life in the later part of the 19thC. The collection was given to Denmark by the tobacco manufacturer, Heinrich Hirschsprung. See MUSEUMS 1.

Hovedbanegård: Copenhagen's Central Station (off Vesterbrogade). Trains leave from here for destinations all over Denmark and Europe. It is also an S-train station and is large and busy with many facilities including toilets (with showers), left-luggage lockers and office, a post office (see A-Z), banks (see **Money**), a supermarket which is open till 2400 seven days a week, a police station and a Room Service kiosk which helps find accommodation in the city (see **Accommodation**). It also has a large selection of restaurants, cafés, and fast-food kiosks with buses and taxi ranks outside in Bernstorffsgade. See **Railways**.

Insurance: You should take out travel insurance covering you against theft and loss of property and money, as well as medical expenses, for the duration of your stay. Your travel agent should be able to recommend a suitable policy. See **Crime & Theft**, **Driving**, **Health**.

Jens Olsen's World Clock: This astronomical clock in the Rådhus (see **BUILDINGS**, **A-Z**) shows world times and the courses of stars and planets as well as the dates in both the Julian and Gregorian calendars.

Jernbanemuseet (Railway Museum): Illustrates the history of Danish railways with a collection of model locomotives, old railway carriages and other memorabilia. The musuem is at Sølvgade 40 (1200-1500 Sat. only (May-Oct.); bus 10, 24, 43, 84; free).

Karetmuseet (Carriage Museum): This exhibition of royal coaches, livery, etc. from the late 18thC is set on the south side of the Riding Ground (Christiansborg Ridebane 33), in one of the wings of the first Christiansborg Slot (see **A-Z**) which survived two fires. Open 1400-1600 Fri.-Sun. (May-Oct.); 5kr, child 2kr.

Kastellet (Citadel): Lying close to Langelinie (see **A-Z**), this large fortress was originally built in the first half of the 17thC to fortify Copenhagen. The Citadel was protected by bastions, two sets of earthworks and a moat, which can still be seen today. See **WALK 1**.

Kierkegaard, Søren (1813-55): A philosopher and poet who argued that we can live on three different levels – aesthetic, ethical and religious. His philosophy influenced existentialist theory. See **WALK 3**.

Kongelige Teater: The Royal Theatre, set on Kongens Nytorv (see **SQUARES**, **A-Z**), is one of the most important theatre venues in Copenhagen. It has three stages – the Old, the New and the Greyfriars Stage – and drama, opera and ballet are all performed here Mon.-Sat. every week during the season (Sep.-May). For advance booking, tel: 31141765 (1200-1700).

Kongens Nytorv: Laid out by Christian V, but planned by Christian IV (see **A-Z**) as the link between the old and the new Copenhagen, Kongens Nytorv was the first royal square in Copenhagen and was surrounded by elegant mansions belonging to the noblest and wealthiest families of the city. Some of these houses are still standing – two of the most notable being Charlottenborg Slot (see **A-Z**) and Thotts Palais (now the French Embassy). The square's most impressive building is that of the Kongelige Teater (see **A-Z**), flanked by statues of the dramatists Ludwig Holberg and Adam Oehlenschläger. See **SQUARES**, **WALK 4**.

Kunstindustrimuseet: See **MUSEUMS 1**, **WALK 4**.

Lakes: Three man-made lakes, split into five sections, stretch from Gammel Kongevej, just a few minutes' walk from Rådhuspladsen (see **SQUARES**), past the new Planetarium, to Østerbrogade. A very pleasant couple of hours can be spent strolling here, enjoying a completely different view of the city. Boats can be hired at Peblinge Sø.

Langelinie: A long promenade created at the end of the 18thC, when the citizens of Copenhagen were granted permission to walk in the area around Kastellet (see **A-Z**) and the outer earthworks. This walk was known as Langelinie or 'The Long Line'. The whole of Langelinie park was laid out at the end of the 1890s, and since then many monuments and sculptures have been added, the most famous being the Little Mermaid (see **A-Z**). See **PARKS & GARDENS**, **WALK 1**.

Laundries: All over the city, there are self-service, coin-operated laundrettes – look for signs saying *Vaskeriet* or *Mønt Vask*. Allow between 40-50kr for one complete washing.

Legoland

Legoland: This entertainment park in Billund, on Jutland, was opened in 1968 by Lego System A/C. Legoland is 238 km from Copenhagen and a visit means a journey by car, train or coach, plus a short ferry journey. Trains to Billund leave from Copenhagen Central Station and bus tours are available (see **Tourist Information**). Thirty-five million Lego bricks were used to create buildings from all over the world. The various other attractions include Fairytale Land, based on the stories of the Brothers Grimm; an indoor exhibition of antique toys, a Lego exhibition, plus a shop and café (1000-1700 mid-April to mid-Dec.; 20kr, child 10kr); a restaurant and hotel; funfair rides, a mini-railway, monorail, etc. (1000-1700, 1000-1930 in the high season). The season for Legoland begins on 28 April and ends on the second Sun. in Sep. (1000-2000, till 2100 from 23 June-12 Aug.). The cost of entry is 40kr, child 20kr. An *Aktivitets Kort* (special price of 28kr in May & Sep.) gives half-price entry to a choice of eight of Legoland's attractions (funfair rides, mini-railway, monorail, etc.). Tel: 75331333 for information.

Little Mermaid (Den Lille Havfrue): Hans Christian Andersen's (see **Andersen**) tragic little heroine, modelled in bronze by Edvard Eriksen in 1913, can be seen from the Langelinie (see **A-Z**). Ballerina

Ellen Price, who had danced the role of the Little Mermaid in a ballet, posed as a model for the statue. In past years, the Mermaid has been vandalized, at different times having her head and one arm chopped off. Thankfully, the original moulds still remain and new casts can be taken. See **WALK 1**.

Lost Property Offices:
Copenhagen Police: Carl Jacobsebsvej 20, 2500 Valby, tel: 31161406 (1000-1500 Mon.-Fri., till 1700 Thu.).
Frederiksberg Police, Hittegodskontoret (Lost Property Office), Solbjergvej 39, 2000 Frederiksberg, tel: 31191448 (1000-1500 Mon.-Fri., till 1800 Thu.).
Buses – Rådhus (Town Hall), Rådhuspladsen, tel: 31124076 (0600-1800 Mon.-Fri., 1000-1400 Sat.).
Trains – Lyshøjgaardsveg 80 (at Valby station) (1000-1800 Mon.-Fri., 0830-1200 Sat.).
Airlines – Copenhagen Airport, Kastrup, tel: 31503211 (0700-2200).

Markets: The only regular markets in Copenhagen are the Flea Market, held in Israel Plads (see **SQUARES**) every Saturday, May-Sep. and Grøntorvet – on Frederiksborggade, backing onto Israel Plads – a large fruit, vegetable and flower market comprised of many different stalls which is open every day. Otherwise, in the larger squares there are often fruit and flower stalls, and in the summer street vendors set out their wares on stands or often just rugs spread out on the ground.

Marmor Bro: At one time the main entrance to Christiansborg Slot (see **A-Z**), the Marble Bridge spans the canal waters to connect Slotsholmen with Frederiksholms Kanal, just beside the Nationalmuseet (see **A-Z**). See **WALK 3**.

Marmor Kirke: The Marble Church, or Frederiks Kirke, was in the original 18thC plan for Frederiksstaden (see **A-Z**) but was not completed until 1894. It is made mostly of Norwegian marble and the 16 statues round the rim of the huge dome (inspired by St. Peter's in Rome) are apostles, prophets or modern religious visionaries. See **WALK 4**.

Money: Normal opening hours for banks are 0930-1600 Mon.-Fri., till 1800 Thu. The following banks have longer opening hours: Copenhagen Handelsbank, Central Railway Station, 0700-2100 1 Oct.-14 April; 0645-2200 15 April-30 Sep.; Den Danske Bank, Tivoli (in season), 1200-2300; Copenhagen Handelsbank, Østergade 26, 0900-1730 Mon.-Wed., 0900-1800 Thu., Fri., 0900-1400 Sat.; Den Danske Bank, Copenhagen Airport, Kastrup, 0630-2200 seven days; American Express, Amagertorv 18, 0900-1700 Mon., Tue., Thu., Fri., 0930-1700 Wed., 0900-1200 Sat. Banks will give the best exchange rate, and all give the same. You are advised not to change money in your hotel as you will be charged extra for this service. Around the city, you will see red-and-white Kontanten cash machines and Visa and Eurocheque cards can be used at these. In general, personal cheques cannot be used. However, the American Express office on Strøget (Amagertorv 18) will accept a personal cheque covered by a valid American Express card. Most major credit cards are accepted by hotels, restaurants, department stores and specialist shops in the city centre. Many shops accept traveller's cheques and banks and savings banks will also cash Eurocheques and traveller's cheques. If you lose a Eurocard, Visa, Mastercard/Access or Eurocheque, contact Eurocard Denmark, tel: 42658866 (0700-2400). See **Currency**.

Music: Opera and ballet are performed in the Royal Theatre (see **Kongelige Teater**) at Kongens Nytorv (see **A-Z**) from Sep.-May. Performances usually begin at 2000 and the theatre is closed on Sundays. To book tickets, tel: 31141765 (1200-1700), or contact ticket agencies (see **Tourist Information**). For information about all music performances or tickets contact Dansk Musik Information Center, Vimmelskaften 48, tel: 31112066. Also check *Copenhagen This Week* (see **What's On**). Tivoli Concert Hall (see **Tivoli**) provides a full programme of musical events through the summer. You can book tickets in advance at the office beside the main entrance to Tivoli, on Vesterbrogade, or tel: 33151012 (1200-2000). Live music, folk, jazz and blues are performed in bars and cafés all over the city, and the highlight of the jazz year comes with the Copenhagen Jazz Festival in July (details from Dansk Musik Information Center). See **NIGHTLIFE**.

Musikhistorisk Museum: A large and varied collection of historical musical instruments as well as a library of musical history. The museum is at Åbenrå 30 (1000-1300 Tue., Wed., 1300-1600 Fri., Sat., Sun.; S-train to Nørreport; bus 5, 7, 14, 16; 15kr, child 3kr).

Nationalmuseet: The National Historical Museum of Denmark, also containing a large Oriental and Classical department and a substantial Ethnographic collection. Other interesting exhibitions include the Danish Folk Museum and the Royal collection of coins and medals. There is a free museum guide available at the information desk on the ground floor. Check *Copenhagen This Week* (see **What's On**) for details of guided tours in English. See **MUSEUMS 1, WALK 3.**

Newspapers: British and other foreign newspapers can be bought in several places in the city centre, e.g. at kiosks in Rådhuspladsen (see **SQUARES**), Jorcks Passage (just off Strøget), Central Station (see **Hovedbanegård**) and in department stores such as Illum and Magasin (see **SHOPPING 1**). See **What's On**.

Nightlife: Nightbirds will find plenty to choose from. Late-night bars are often open until after 0200, and many until 0500. Discos vary from dressy to very informal, but you will have to pay an entrance fee at all of them. Most are open 2200-0500. Nightclubs provide entertainment such as live music, cabaret, dancing and meals and their clientele is usually older and affluent, enjoying a comfortable and sophisticated atmosphere and paying fees and charges to match. The other side of nightlife is the red-light district, in Vesterbro, near the city centre and close to the large hotels, around Vesterbrogade and Istedgade. It is a sad district frequented by many of the street people with drink and drug problems. You will not be under any threat here but women on their own should avoid this area. See **NIGHTLIFE**.

Ny Carlsberg Glyptotek: Built to house the art collection of Carl and Ottila Jacobsen (of Carlsberg Breweries) and donated to the Danish state in 1888. There are two buildings joined by a conservatory filled with palms, a fountain, and statues. The Antiquities section of the museum contains work from the Etruscan, Greek, Roman and Egyptian civilizations. The modern section contains a collection of the French Impressionists, including a set of Degas' bronze statuettes, and a large selection of the work of Paul Gauguin. There are also sections devoted to the sculptures of Rodin, Danish Golden Age painting and Russian and Greek iconography. See **MUSEUMS 1**.

Nyhavn: The canal at Nyhavn was dug in 1671, to provide access for ships to Kongens Nytorv (see **SQUARES**). The tall houses which now line the canal on both sides were built in the 17th-18thC by the merchants trading from and around the canal. At the end of the 19thC, the two sides of Nyhavn had very different reputations. The south side was gen-teel and respectable, while the north side was the sailors' quarter, with rowdy bars, street brawls, prostitutes and pickpockets. In the 1950s and '60s, artists and other Bohemian figures began to use the area so that gradually it became more acceptable. Today, Nyhavn is a colourful and fashionable area and one of the liveliest spots in town – particularly during the summer months. In good weather large groups of people can be found sitting outside bars alongside the canal, drinking beer and watching the world go by. The large anchor at the beginning of Nyhavn is from the frigate *Fyn*, and was placed here in memory of the Danish sailors who lost their lives during World War II. See **WALK 4**, **Events**.

Opening Times: In general:
Banks – 0930-1600 Mon.-Fri., till 1800 Thu.
Lost Property Office (police) – 1000-1500 Mon.-Fri., till 1700 Thu.
Post Office – (main office) 0800-1900 Mon.-Fri., 0900-1300 Sat.
Shops – 0900-1730 Mon.-Thu., 0900-1900/2000 Fri., 0900-1300 Sat.

Orientation: The centre of Copenhagen is very compact, with Rådhuspladsen (see **SQUARES**) being the focal point and most of what you will want to see nearby. The city is divided into four distinct areas. The centre comprises the Old City, Frederiksstaden (see **WALK 4**) and Christianshavn (see **A-Z**) on the island of Amager (see **A-Z**), just across the harbour channel. The second area is the Rampart Quarters, of Vesterbro, Østerbro and Nørrebro, which were built outside the original walls of the city. The third area is Frederiksberg, and the fourth is the outer ring of districts which have gradually been absorbed into the Greater Copenhagen area – Emdrup, Bispebjerg, Brønshøj, Husum, Vanløse, Valby and Sundby.

Parking: As in any city, parking is limited in business hours during the week. Payment for space (0800-1700 Mon.-Fri., 0800-1400 Sat.) is by disks or tickets from dispensing machines (*billetautomat*). Tickets cost 15kr (max. 3 hr). Car-hire firms (see **Car Hire**) have information on multi-storey car parks. If you park illegally you could be fined or have your car towed away. If this happens contact the nearest police station (see **Police**). You will have to pay 300kr to retrieve your car.

Passports & Customs: You must have a valid passport, and for a stay of more than three months you will also need a visa. If in doubt check with your country's Danish embassy. There are no restrictions on the amount of money being brought into the country, but if you should leave with any large amounts (max. 50,000Dkr), this should be declared on re-entering your own country. See **Customs Allowances**.

Petrol: Sold by the litre (98 octane is the four-star equivalent) with lead-free (*bly-fri*) and diesel available at most filling stations. The majority of filling stations are self-service and opening times vary, although they are often open until 2000 or 2200.

Police: Danish police wear a very dark navy-blue uniform and their cars are dark blue and white or all white, and marked with *Politi*. If you need help do not hesitate to stop an officer or a car or go into a police station – all police speak excellent English. The main police station, Politigården, Polititorvet, is open 24 hr, seven days, tel: 33141448. See **Crime & Theft**, **Emergency Number**.

Post Offices: Normal opening hours are 0900/1000-1700/1730 Mon.-Fri., 0900-1200 Sat. The main office is at Tietgensgade 37 (0800-1900 Mon.-Fri., 0900-1300 Sat.), and there is an office in Central Station (0800-2200 Mon.-Fri., 0900-1800 Sat., 1000-1700 Sun.). It costs 3.5kr to send letters (up to 20g) within Europe, airmail (20g) and postcards, while letters and cards elsewhere cost 4.5kr. Facilities at the main office include a poste restante service and telex. Money can be sent to or collected at any post office. See **Telephones & Telegrams**.

Public Holidays: 1 Jan. (New Year's Day); Maundy Thursday; Good Friday; Easter Monday; General Prayers Day (four weeks after Easter); Ascension Day; Whit Monday; 5 June (Constitution Day); 25 Dec. (Christmas Day); 26 Dec. (Boxing Day). See **Events**.

Rabies: This disease infects many wild animals and some domestic animals; have all animal bites treated by a doctor. See **Health**.

Rådhus: The present Town Hall is the city's sixth and the best way to see this Italianate building is to take a guided tour, including a climb to the top of the 106-m-high tower. There are five bells above the clock which ring the quarter, half and full hours. The figures along the roof ridge are town watchmen in the official uniforms of different eras and the gilded statue above the entrance is Bishop Absalon, the city's founder. Inside is Jens Olsen's World Clock (see **A-Z**). See **BUILDINGS**.

Rådhuspladsen: See SQUARES, **Orientation**.

Railways: Copenhagen's S-train service is an electrified system which links the city and suburbs. Trains are frequent (every 10 or 20 min, more frequent in rush hours) and the service is good. Carriages are clean and most are non-smoking. You can pick up timetables at stations and maps of the network are available on platforms, in carriages, inside *Copenhagen This Week* (see **What's On**), from the Tourist Information office, travel agencies and some hotels. Tickets are bought at ticket counters (*Billetter* or *Billet Salg*). If you have a discount ticket (see **Transport**) it must be clipped before you board. Children under 12 pay half fare, and under fives travel free. A list of destinations beside the clipping machines tells you how many clips are needed for your journey. If an inspector finds you have an unclipped ticket you may be fined on the spot. Doors on S-trains open only when you press lightly on the door handle. Trains start running at 0500 (0600 Sun.), and the last trains are at around 0030. The main S-train stations are Central Station (see **Hovedbanegård**), Westerport, Nørreport and Østerport. Trains to North Zealand or other parts of Denmark leave from the Central Station. The ticket office is just inside the main entrance and posters give timetables. Platforms have clear signs giving destinations, stops en route and departure times. See **Copenhagen Card**, **Transport**.

Religious Services: There are English-language services at the following places: St. Alban's Anglican Episcopalian Church, Churchill-parken, Langelinie; The American Church of Copenhagen, Farvergade 27; Jesu Hjerte Kirke (RC), Stenosgade 4; and Hebrew services in the Synagogue, Krystalgade 12. See **CHURCHES**.

Rosenborg Slot: This beautiful palace is set in Kongens Have (see **PARKS & GARDENS**) and contains the royal museum where the crown jewels are on display. See **MUSEUMS 2**, **Amalienborg Slot**.

Roskilde: 35 km west of Copenhagen. Pop: 49,000. Train to Roskilde Station. This historic university town has many attractions for the visitor including the 12thC Cathedral, Viking Ship Museum and Roskilde Museum. See **EXCURSION 3**.

Rundetårn: The Round Tower and observatory is one of the best-known city landmarks. The Tower was part of the original Trinitatis Kirke (see **CHURCHES**) and its spiral ramp was designed to allow heavy astronomical equipment to reach the observatory at the top. There is an exhibition area which is entered from half-way up the tower and wonderful views over the city from the top. See **BUILDINGS**.

Scala: A large shopping and restaurant complex on the block between Vesterbrogade and Axeltorv. As well as a great variety of shops there are more than 20 cafés and restaurants, some with pavement and roof-top terraces, offering many different cuisines and fast-food services. See **Shopping**.

Shopping: Copenhagen is an excellent shopping city and all the best shopping areas are right in the centre. The main shopping area is Strøget – the 'walking street' – running from Rådhuspladsen to Kongens Nytorv (see **SQUARES**) along Fredericksberggade, Nygade, Vimmelskaftet, Amagertorv and Østergade. You can buy just about anything on Strøget – a souvenir T-shirt or fur coat, jewellery or an ice-cream. As this area can get extremely busy in the summer, it is a good idea to walk along the parallel streets on either side where there are smaller, specialist shops. It is worth noting that some food shops in the city may close on Mon. or Tue. but there is a supermarket in Central Station which is open until midnight including Sun. In Denmark VAT is known as MOMS and charged at 22% on all goods and services. Look out for Tax Free shops where you can have the tax on purchases of not less than 2800kr refunded before leaving Denmark, or arrange to have the goods sent to your home. There is an 18% reduction on the tax and you pay postage and insurance. See **SHOPPING**, **Scala**.

Slotsholmen: See **Christiansborg Slot**, **WALK 3**.

Smoking: Smoking and non-smoking areas are indicated on trains and in many restaurants and cafés. There is no smoking on buses, in theatre auditoriums, cinemas, museums or on any SAS flights within Denmark and Scandinavia. See **Best Buys**.

Søfartsmonument: This striking winged figure at the beginning of Langelinie (see **PARKS & GARDENS**) was erected to the memory of the Danish sailors who lost their lives during World War I. See **WALK 1**.

Sport: For information on sporting events such as cycle racing, football, horse racing, etc. ask at the Tourist Information office (see **Tourist Information**), see the yellow centre pages of *Copenhagen This Week* (see **What's On**) or contact Idrætsparken, the main stadium, which provides an information service on all sporting events, tel: 31426860 (0800-1600 Mon.-Fri.). Participator sports:

Bowling – Bryggens Bowling Centre, Islands Brygge 83 (1600-2300 Mon.-Fri., 1300-1800 Sat., 1000-1800 Sun.; bus 40; 98kr per hr).

Fishing – Søllerød Naturpark, Langkærdammen on Attemosevej, Holte. You will need a licence for freshwater fishing (available from Jagt ot Fiskermagasinet, Frederiksberg Allé 27) and your own tackle.

There is no licence required for sea fishing, but bring your own tackle. For boat hire contact: M/S Arresø, Kalkbranderihavn, tel: 31570724; M/S Skipper, Tuborg Havn Syd, Hellerup, tel: 31181038.

Golf – for information contact Dansk Golf Union, Bredgade 56, 1260 København, tel: 31131221. Guests are welcome at clubs in the Copenhagen area. Bring your club membership. Golf club hire.
Horse riding – Sports Riding Club, Maltagårdsvej, Gentofte (S-train to Bernstorffsvej).
Tennis – Københavns Boldklub, Peter Bangsvej 147, 2000 Frederiksberg, tel: 31714150. Courts are always busy, so book ahead.
Skating – Østerbro Skøjterhal, Per Henrik Lings Allé 6, tel: 31262946.
Swimming – Emdrup Svømmehal, Bredelandsvej 20; Frederiksberg Svømmehal, Helgesvej 29; Vesterbro Svømmehal, Angelgade 4.

Statens Museum for Kunst (Royal Museum of Fine Art):
The approach to this impressive building, designed in the Italian Renaissance style, is dominated by a curious crescent-shaped wall, topped by a series of multi-coloured figures – this is 'The Human Wall' by Danish artist, Bjørn Nørgaard. The museum covers Danish and European art from the 14thC to the present. As well as showing the work of contemporary Danish artists, you can also see works by Rembrandt, Picasso, Matisse and Edvard Munch. The museum has a small cafeteria in the basement. See MUSEUMS 2.

Strøget: See SHOPPING, **Shopping**.

Taxis: Taxis are saloon cars, easily recognizable by the green 'Taxi' sign, and horizontal stripes painted on the side of the car. They display a green 'Fri' sign in the windscreen when available. There are ranks at Central Station (see **Hovedbanegård**), Kongens Nytorv, Rådhuspladsen (see SQUARES), and in various other spots around the city, and cars can be hailed in the street. The basic fare is 12kr but will be up to 30% more expensive after 0100 and at weekends. See **Tipping**.

Telephones & Telegrams: Telephone kiosks are grey and can be found all over the city. The phones take 25 øre, 1kr and 5kr coins. A phone-card system is gradually being introduced with cards of 20kr and 90kr available. There are graphic instructions for use of the phones inside the kiosks. You can make international calls by dialling direct from all telephone booths in the city – dial 009 followed by the national code (UK: 44), the area code (minus the first zero) and the personal number. Copenhagen city centre and the inner suburbs have the code 31, outer suburbs are mostly 42, the rest of Zealand 53, followed by six digits. Directory Enquires (local/international) – 0033/0039; Operator (Denmark/international) – 0011/0015.

Telegrams can be sent by phone and from telex boxes (tel: 0022; for information tel: 0028) or from any post office (see **Post Offices**). The Telecom Centre in Central Station, Verterbrogade, has Fax and telex facilities (0900-2000 Mon.-Fri., 0900-1600 Sat., 1000-1700 Sun.).

Television & Radio: Danish television has two national stations – Danmarks Radio is the state-run television channel broadcasting every day from 1545-2330 and TV2 is a privately-owned channel broadcasting every day from 1800-2400. Both channels present a mix of home-produced and imported programmes, and any English-language programmes have sub-titles. Two Swedish channels are also available, again with the same mix of programmes. Satellite TV has many channels available, including Cable News Network. Most of the large hotels can offer a selection of cable and satellite channels, as well as the normal Danish and Swedish channels.

Danmarks Radio offers three radio channels. Radio 1 (0600-2300 – news, magazine programmes and drama; 0810 Mon.-Sat, also Sun. Sep.-April – news in English). Radio 2 (0530-1930 – regional services; 1930-2330 – classical music). Radio 3 (24 hr – easy listening). As well as the state-run stations there are many local radio stations – in the Copenhagen area alone there are between 10 and 15 different frequencies – and you can pick up every kind of rock, pop and jazz music.

Thorvaldsens Museum: This striking neoclassical building was built to house the works of Danish sculptor Bertel Thorvaldsen (1770-1844). Thorvaldsen lived in Rome 1797-1838, and took his inspiration from Greek and Roman antiquities. The yellow, red-ochre and black frieze around the outside of the building depicts Thorvaldsen's return to Copenhagen from Rome in 1838. He is buried in the courtyard of the building. See **MUSEUMS 2, WALK 3**.

Time Difference: Denmark is 1 hour ahead of GMT. In summer the clocks go forward 1 hour, keeping Denmark 1 hour ahead of BST.

Tipping: Tipping is not generally expected and there are no hard-and-fast rules. In restaurants and cafés, you will normally find that service has been added to the bill. It is up to you to decide whether extra is deserved. The same applies to taxis.

Tivoli: To many people who have never visited the city, the one thing they know of in Copenhagen is Tivoli. This pleasure garden is almost 100 years old and is still packed every night. The management boast that there is no plastic and not one neon bulb in Tivoli. Water, light and flowers everywhere are among the ingredients which make Tivoli so special, and if you don't want to try the hair-raising fairground rides you will enjoy strolling in the gardens, watching the various perfor-mances or having a meal in one of the many restaurants. The

Pantomime Theatre has performances every evening; there is music at the bandstands; the open-air stage has daily variety performances; there is a children's theatre; folk music in the Vise-Vers-Muset; jazz in the Jazzhus Slukefter and the Tivoli Revue every evening in the Glass Hall. There are fireworks displays on Wed. and Sat., and on Fri. after June, at 2330 from the open-air stage, and on Sun. at 2330 from the lake. There is also a children's play area and a picnic area by the lake (cutlery, plates and glasses for your picnic can be hired), a bank, a post office and an information centre (1200-2300). There is so much to see and do you will want to come back again and again. See **CHILDREN**, **Copenhagen Card**.

Toilets: In general, public toilets in Copenhagen are clean and well looked after – and in some cases they are surprisingly good. Central Station (see **Hovedbanegård**) has large facilities, with showers. There are also public toilets in Nyhavn (see **A-Z**), in Rådhuspladsen, underneath Amagertorv, in the large department stores such as Illum and Magasin (see **SHOPPING 1**) and in the S-train stations (see **Railways**). Many of the larger public toilets also provide baby changing facilities.

Tourist Information: The Tourist Information office (Danish Tourist Board) is at H. C. Andersen Boulevard 22, by Rådhuspladsen, tel: 33111325. It is open 0900-1800 Mon.-Fri., 0900-1400 Sat. (1 May-30 Sep.); 0900-1700 Mon.-Fri., 0900-1200 Sat. (1 Oct-30 April); closed Sun. & hol. The staff offer extensive help and information on all aspects of visiting Copenhagen and North Zealand, and a wide range of free brochures and leaflets is available. Bookings can also be made for tours and excursions and staff can provide advance information for entertainment. Danvisit is located in the same building, and information on accommodation (see **A-Z**) can be obtained there. All staff speak English, and are generally very helpful, although in the high season they are also extremely busy. If you want information before travelling, contact The Danish Tourist Board, UK Office, Sceptre House, 169-173 Regent Street, London W1R 8PY. See **Copenhagen Card**, **What's On**.

Transport: A joint tariff system is used for all HT-buses and S-trains within the metropolitan area. Tickets and discount tickets allow you to transfer between trains and buses within specific areas (zones) and certain time limits. Tickets are valid for 1 hr in three zones, 1 hr 30 min in four-six zones and 2 hr in seven or more zones. Tickets cost from 8-32kr and can be bought on buses or at railway stations. It is worth buying a *Rabatkort* or discount ticket, which will cover ten journeys. There are three grades of discount ticket, costing 70kr, 125kr and 190kr depending on which of the three zones you require. These can be bought at railway stations, and the 70kr ticket can also be bought on buses. For a tourist travelling around the city, and with possibly a couple of train journeys outside, a 70kr ticket is probably all that is necessary. Children up to 12 years old pay half price. See **Buses**, **Copenhagen Card**, **Railways**.

Traveller's Cheques: See Money.

Tuborg Brewery: Founded in 1873, this famous brewery offers tours and free samples of beer. It is located at Strandvejen 54, Hellerup, tel: 31293311 (1000, 1230, 1430 Mon.-Fri., or by special arrangement; bus 1, 21; free).

Tycho Brahe Planetarium: This is one of the newest attractions in Copenhagen, offering the chance to explore the universe with the aid of the most advanced equipment. It is named after the astronomer Tycho Brahe (1546-1601) who discovered a new star within the constellation Cassiopeia, in 1572. The planetarium is housed in a striking building with an angled roof beside the lake on Gammel Kongevej, with a restaurant and lakeside café.

University: Founded in 1479, the present building in Frue Plads (see SQUARES) dates from the early 1830s. It was built on the site of the old university, which was destroyed by the 1807 bombardment during the Napoleonic Wars.

Vikings: The Viking period spans the last part of the Nordic Iron Age, from AD 800-1050. The period was marked by wide expansion of the Scandinavian peoples – both east and west – as the Vikings voyaged across the sea, conquering in many lands, including the Faroe Islands, Iceland, Greenland, parts of the north-west European coasts and the British Isles. The Danes relish this period of their history – especially the fact that at one time England was ruled by a Danish king, King Canute (Orknud) from 1016-35. Viking society was dominated by a rich and arrogant upper class whose power was based on the ownership of land, and on family solidarity. Rich burial grounds bear witness to the highly-developed skills in the arts and crafts which they applied to weapons, ornaments and jewellery. To find out more about the Vikings, and especially their ships and voyages, visit the Viking Ship Museum at Roskilde – set beside Roskilde Fjord, where the ships on display were discovered (see EXCURSION 3). In Copenhagen, the Nationalmuseet (see MUSEUMS 1) has many Viking artefacts – jewellery, weapons, helmets, etc.

Vor Frelsers Kirke: The spiral tower of this late-17thC baroque church, 75m high with an outside spiral staircase, is one of the most distinctive features of the Copenhagen skyline. It culminates in a large gilt ball, on top of which stands a figure of Christ holding a banner. There is a magnificent view from the top of the tower, but the ascent is not for the fainthearted. See **CHURCHES**, **WALK 2**.

Vor Frue Kirke (Our Lady's Church/Cathedral): This neoclassical church, designed by C. F. Hansen, was built between 1811-29, and is arguably the loveliest church in the city, with its white walls, the simplest of lighting and the superb sculptures by Bertel Thorvaldsen – the twelve apostles lining the way from the door to the altar and Christ above the altar. The font was also designed by Thorvaldsen, as were the bronze statues of Moses and David which stand on either side of the church entrance. See **CHURCHES**.

What's On: The only regular publication which covers all events in the city is the English-language *Copenhagen This Week*, free and available from Tourist Information (see **A-Z**), hotels, travel agencies, shops and cafés around the city. All the main newspapers – particularly *Berlingske Tidende* and *Politiken* – have excellent listings for theatre, concerts, exhibitions, films, etc. every day, with the Friday issue giving complete details on everything happening over the weekend including a restaurant guide, a list of sports events, etc. Also available from Tourist Information, free, is *Tourist in Copenhagen and North Zealand*. See **Music**, **Events**.

Youth Hostels: There is very little risk in Denmark of finding accommodation for young people which is not of a decent standard – the Danes set great store by being organized and clean. You will need a Danish or International Youth Hostels Association membership card.

A Danish membership or a guest card can be bought at the hostels (Danish card – 90kr, guest card – 18kr). In Copenhagen try: Danmarks Vandrehjem, Vesterbrogade 39, 1620 Copenhagen V, tel: 31313612 or Vesterbro Ungdomsgård, Absalonsgade 8 (95kr per night, incl. breakfast). A free brochure, *Youth Hostels,* can be obtained at the Tourist Information office, and at the offices of the Danish Tourist Board in the UK (see **Tourist Information**). The official guide can be bought from Danmarks Vandrehjem. Young people could also try Copenhagen Sleep-In, Per Henrik Lings Allé 6, 2100 København 0, tel: 3125059 (27 June-1 Sep.). Accommodation is in large dormitories, and the cost is about 50kr per night. It is best to phone first. See **Accommodation**.

Zoologisk Have (Zoological Gardens): A pleasant and well laid out zoo with all the expected animals – big cats, bears, elephants, as well as many smaller species, and many different birds. The settings

echo the animals' natural habitat as much as possible. There is a restaurant and plenty of fast food and drinks on offer. See **CHILDREN**.

Zoologisk Museum: An excellent museum for children with tableaux depicting animals, birds, fish and insect life in reconstructions of their natural habitats. There is a special section on the wildlife of Denmark, and an excellent marine exhibit with life-size models of whales and giant squid, as well as 'Pole to Pole' tableaux of how animals live, from the Arctic, via temperate, tropical and desert environments, to the Antarctic. Earphones allow you to listen to the sounds of the African bush, or a tropical rain forest. There is a cafeteria and a small souvenir shop in the museum. See **CHILDREN**.